THE SCIENTIST ENTREPRENEUR

'*The Scientist Entrepreneur* is not just a narrative of Dr Kalpana Sankar's journey but a source of inspiration for aspiring entrepreneurs, academicians and philanthropists and a valuable resource for a diverse global audience. This fascinating book contributes significantly to the broader narrative of social entrepreneurship and empowerment, making it a must-read for those seeking to make a positive socioeconomic impact globally.'

—Kiran Mazumdar-Shaw
Executive Chairperson, Biocon Limited and Biocon Biologics Limited

'Dr Kalpana Sankar's life has been an extraordinary journey characterized by resilience, ambition and a commitment to social impact. It will inspire young men and women to become social entrepreneurs and touch the lives of millions.'

—Soumya Swaminathan
Former Chief Scientist, World Health Organization (WHO) and
Chairperson, M.S. Swaminathan Research Foundation

'This is a fascinating book that weaves together the powerful story of a woman leader who is passionate and results-oriented, yet empathetic and humble at the same time. Amazing story. So many lessons to be learnt for modern women who want to make a difference in the world on their terms. Women can do it all. Kalpana Sankar is an inspiring example.'

—V. Kasturi Rangan
Baker Foundation Professor, Harvard Business School

'In a world where individuals and companies talk the "social impact" talk, but are unable or unwilling to walk the "social impact" walk, Kalpana stands out as someone who couples passion for change with a willingness to work to deliver that change. Hand in Hand, her co-creation, has not only scaled up successfully, stretching beyond its Indian origins, but has done so without compromising its ideals or vision, thanks to her.'

—Aswath Damodaran
Kerschner Family Chair in Finance Education and
Professor of Finance, New York University Stern School of Business

'Kalpana is amongst India's pioneers in adopting water and sanitation as a financial product. Since 2009, under her leadership, Hand in Hand has ensured that people living at the base of the economic pyramid have access to safe water and clean toilets in their households.'

—Gary White
CEO and Co-founder, Water.org and WaterEquity

'The book narrates the journey of Dr Kalpana, who co-founded the organization Hand in Hand (HIH) in 2004, dedicated to child development and welfare. Dr Kalpana's story is depicted through her experiences, challenges and achievements, highlighting the impact of HIH in transforming the lives of underprivileged children and families in India. It is an inspiring journey of creating positive change and empowering communities.'

—Manika Raikwar
Former Managing Editor, NDTV

THE SCIENTIST ENTREPRENEUR

Empowering Millions of Women

KALPANA SANKAR

RUPA

Published by
Rupa Publications India Pvt. Ltd 2024
7/16, Ansari Road, Daryaganj
New Delhi 110002

Sales centres:
Bengaluru Chennai Hyderabad
Jaipur Kathmandu Kolkata
Mumbai Prayagraj

P-ISBN: 978-93-6156-040-8
E-ISBN: 978-93-6156-411-6

Second impression 2024

10 9 8 7 6 5 4 3 2

Printed in India

This book is dedicated to

my Guru, Bhagwan Sri Sathya Sai Baba;

my parents;
my sisters, Bindu & Kamini;

my husband, Sankar;
my daughter, Sahaana; and

my close friends—Mali, Ramani and Mihoko

CONTENTS

FOREWORD

Over the years, I have had the privilege of recruiting many talented individuals across various companies all over the world. However, I believe the most important one was of Kalpana Sankar to lead Hand in Hand some 20 years ago. A doctorate in Theoretical Nuclear Physics, Kalpana not only possessed a brilliant mind but was also driven by an urge to improve the situation for millions of poor women and their families.

We had a saying at Hand in Hand—'do not give a poor person a fish; give them a fishing rod instead.' Kalpana turned this philosophy into reality. A mass mobilization of poor people into entrepreneurship started to change the way aid was organized in the world.

Training programmes, particularly for women, and microfinance to provide lending support started in Tamil Nadu and gradually spread to other Indian states. Under the Hand in Hand banner, this approach to poverty alleviation spread to countries like Afghanistan and across African nations like Kenya, Tanzania, Zimbabwe and South Africa.

I explained what Kalpana had accomplished in India to the United Nations (UN) Secretary-General Kofi Annan and leaders of national aid agencies like the Swedish International

Development Cooperation Agency and several others. They were stunned to hear how millions of poor women and their families, with limited financial support, had improved their standards of living. Some initially sceptical aid workers commented on 'the capitalist methods,' but soon became silent when the results were apparent. Thanks to Kalpana's organizational skills and ability to transmit enthusiasm to thousands of Hand in Hand employees, the scale of the results was truly remarkable.

In the beginning, I contributed my expertise from the business world on performance. Looking back over the past two decades, I can safely say that Kalpana, through Hand in Hand, has changed the standard of how to conduct aid work. She recognized the level of untapped potential within impoverished and uneducated women and knew how to release it through entrepreneurship.

I am proud of what Kalpana and her loyal and hardworking employees have achieved. It was certainly way beyond anything I could have imagined 20 years ago. Thanks to her achievements, the world of aid work has attained new dimensions and made a prominent mark on the history of global humanitarian efforts.

—Percy Barnevik

Co-founder, Hand in Hand India

PREFACE

This story is not just about me and my family; it also captures my experiences of working Hand in Hand with marginalized women, children and communities. I started this journey in 2004 and after two decades, I felt the strong desire to document my learnings, hoping they might serve as a beacon of hope and guidance for others.

For me, Hand in Hand is not just another non-governmental organization (NGO); it is a home to some wonderfully passionate individuals who have dedicated their lives to community development. While people on the outside see the impact that Hand in Hand has had on marginalized groups and hear beneficiary stories, this book dives deep into the struggles of building an NGO and a for-profit company successfully, brick by brick. It highlights how we, as a group of organizations, have focussed on our vision of poverty alleviation and community upliftment, especially for women and children, helping them live with renewed faith and dignity. Starting from a small room in Kanchipuram, Tamil Nadu, the organization has expanded its reach across 18 states in India and into countries like Afghanistan, South Africa and Brazil.

In all my transformative experiences, not only have I witnessed abject poverty but also immense hope, which I wish to instil in others through education and empowerment. Another aspect that I have delved deep into is the importance of learning and introspection to create a sustainable enterprise. As a female leader, many of my key decisions were scrutinized by others as people felt I was not cut out to lead the organization.

Is she taking the right step? Isn't she expanding too fast into other countries? Her vision and goals are too lofty and unrealistic; how will she build an NGO aligned with the strategies of a corporate?

Breaking through the metaphorical glass ceiling to emerge as a leader in the NGO and financial inclusion space is a dominant idea I explore through my diverse experiences.

To refine this narrative, I have included incidents from my personal experiences in India and around the world, referencing the copious notes and memos I have prepared over the last 20 years. These anecdotes unveil the duality of running non-profit and corporate organizations with equal synergy and impact.

My aspiration for this book is to inspire young people to embrace entrepreneurship, specifically in the social sector. I hope it instils faith in the next generation, showing them that along with a clear vision, innovation and passion, it takes courage and determination to follow dreams and make a significant difference in the lives of others.

PROLOGUE

KANCHIPURAM TO RASHTRAPATI BHAVAN

22 JANUARY 2019

It was a pleasant winter day with a gentle breeze blowing, which had a soothing effect on all of us. As I walked up the winding path towards the grand entrance of the Rashtrapati Bhavan, I could feel butterflies in my stomach.

'Congratulations Dr Kalpana; your work is truly inspiring,' said Shri Ramnath Kovind, the President of India.

For a moment my mind went blank as this was like a dream come true. I could not believe that I was standing at the residence of the First Citizen of India, who presided over 1.3 billion people. The sheer grandeur, majestic architecture and royal ambience of the place were exquisite. I was there to accept the 'Bal Kalyan Puraskar' on behalf of Hand in Hand (HIH), the organization I co-founded in 2004 in Tamil Nadu, India. This prestigious award honours organizations that create an indelible impact in the field of child development and welfare.

HIH, in its short journey of two decades, has touched the

lives of thousands of women and children, not only in India but in several countries across the world.

My mind raced back to corridors of the past to two years prior when I was in the same Durbar Hall of the Rashtrapati Bhavan to receive the 'Nari Shakti Puraskar' (National Award for Women Empowerment) from the then President of India, Shri Pranab Mukherjee.

Ever so grateful to God, I mentally dedicated these awards to those who had walked alongside me in this journey—my colleagues, the hundreds of volunteers who spread our message to the farthest corners, the philanthropists who enabled the functioning of our NGO on sound professional and ethical grounds, the advisers and Trustees from different fields who mentored me and last but not least, the thousands of women who joined me to empower themselves and their families.

While waiting in the Durbar Hall, I reflected on my journey to the Rashtrapati Bhavan. I couldn't help but recollect how my tryst with HIH started in Kanchipuram at Emma House, a name kept to honour one of our early Swedish donors. The town boasts one of the earliest temples in India—the stone-cut Kailasanathar Temple—built around AD 685–705 by King Narasimhavarman II of the Pallava dynasty. Kanchipuram also takes pride in its thriving handloom industry, which churns out exquisite silk saris. The silk threads are brought all the way from Bangalore (now Bengaluru) and woven into divine patterns by master weavers.

My mind wandered to the people whose lives had been touched by the endeavours of HIH. I thought of Manikandan, who belonged to a family of silk weavers and had to drop out of school in the third grade to help his father weave. Unfortunately, he was one of the few whose life was on mortgage to a rich person as a bonded labourer for a paltry sum borrowed by his parents. Manikandan completed a Diploma in Mechanical Engineering and is now working as an automobile component maker.

The practice of bonded child labour is still quite prevalent in India as children are kept beholden to the lender till the loan is fully paid off by their parents. However, the wages earned by these children do not match that of the adults, prolonging their bondage and depriving them of education.

This was the first issue taken up by HIH. We took baby steps to identify these children, work out the modalities to rescue them from the clutches of debt bondage and bring them back into the fabric of formal education. Each step had to be negotiated slowly. We developed a multipronged approach with short-term and long-term goals to enable a holistic solution. Many of these children had not been exposed to any formal education as their parents saw little value in taking them out of employment; they did not believe in sending them back to school as the children might be forced to return to the same line of work after some time. Just paying off their debts would not eradicate this social evil as it was a temporary fix.

We began our mission with door-to-door surveys where we sent our volunteers to individual households to assess how many children were in school rather than relying on traditional large-scale campaign modes. In the early days, our volunteers, whom we referred to as mobilizers, were typically part-time workers who earned a minimum compensatory sum for their travel and time. Unfortunately, they often were greeted with displeasure and insults during these interactions; physical assaults too were common.

Sukumar and Elumazhai, two of our volunteers, had plates thrown at them when they visited a house to raise awareness. It often took an average of four visits before our messages were heard and elicited responses. Some of the mobilizers also faced hostility from members of the Narikurava tribe (gypsy community). They did not prioritize the education of their children and roamed the streets looking for their next meal and sometimes even pelted stones at our staff.

While the typical NGO culture involved running a few evening classes and offering material donations to underprivileged communities, I knew we needed to do more. Convincing everyone to break free from this toxic cycle, particularly the children who were fundamentally trapped in it, would require considerable time and effort.

Fortunately, I discovered the Mamidipudi Venkatarangaiya Foundation (MVF), a volunteer group that had done some outstanding work for children in Andhra Pradesh. The group went around each village, discreetly identifying children and rescuing them from the clutches of this exploitative practice. They talked to their parents, the lenders and village elders to arrive at practical solutions. These children, who had never gone to school before, were sent to special residential teaching schools, which provided them with a decent place to live, proper food, clothing and their first exposure to books and learning.

The key learning from our partnership with MVF was the importance of adopting the right perspective to understand the problem and its solution. Until then, we approached the villagers as individuals representing HIH, viewing their circumstances as a problem to be solved by us. But once we shifted our mindset and stepped in the villagers' shoes, tackling the issue became easier. We began involving youth from the villages and recruiting them as our mobilizers. We trained them and had them gather basic information, such as the number of out-of-school children or other pertinent school-related data. We also formed a committee comprising a retired school headmaster, the panchayat president and local youth to represent us at the District Collector's office to get more data. Through this inclusive approach, we were able to effectively communicate our message on the importance of education, ensuring that no child was left behind. This process took about six to nine months to evolve as it was imperative that the local community fully accepted us.

❧

HIH has changed the lives of more than 3,50,000 children like Manikandan in the last 20 years, rescuing them from underpaid, exploitative jobs that would have otherwise entrapped them for a long time.[1]

I was clear about a few non-negotiables from the beginning—every child out of school is a child labourer irrespective of whether they worked with their family or outside it. We also wanted to take full advantage of the efforts made by the government and other organizations to advance our mission. Our approach was never to merely replicate the government schemes but rather to address the gaps and add value to the existing system. We believed that there must be full transparency in financial matters and emphasized the importance of integrity being ingrained in each and every employee.

It was imperative that the organization upheld certain basic values at all times. Maintaining these standards might have been easy when the setup was small, but the challenge was sustaining these ethics across multiple initiatives, geographical locations and cultures.

HIH and its group entities have developed a unique model, employing more than 13,229 individuals and working across 18 Indian states, with the experience of having worked in countries like Afghanistan, Brazil, Cambodia, South Africa and Myanmar.[2]

The five pillars of HIH are:

- Child labour elimination and education
- Women's empowerment through microfinance and self-help groups
- Environmental initiatives focussing on natural resource management and solid and liquid waste management
- Health and nutrition programmes
- Skill development and training

Each pillar was seamlessly developed one after another to solve problems holistically and create opportunities for social advancement.

Jeffery Sachs published a book[3] on how to eliminate world poverty, in which he suggested a grant model for uplifting villages in Africa. Early on, given my experience within this sector, I knew that just a grant would not be sufficient for eradicating poverty. We would need a holistic approach—a grant not only for advocacy and knowledge sharing but also training on skills and entrepreneurship, with a focus on education and environment, to bring about lasting change for women, children and communities. Hence, the concept of the Village Uplift Programme (VUP) was conceived. This programme is an umbrella initiative that aims to implement all five pillars in a village to bring about comprehensive need-based development in a compact area. It has been successfully executed in over 400 villages.

For instance, in Kilkadi Panchayat, Tamil Nadu, our interventions over the course of 24 months focussed on areas like child labour elimination, supporting local schools,[4] socioeconomic development of women, microfinance, enterprise development, basic health and personal hygiene, computer literacy, good governance and environmental protection. By the end of this period, 23 self-help groups (SHGs) were formed comprising 276 members, each saving ₹500 per month. These groups were given credit from banks totalling ₹10 lakh, enabling them to grow their enterprises and consequently, their monthly incomes.

Furthermore, the groups progressed to form cluster-level networks (CLNs) to enhance the social capital of the community. The women within these networks actively participated in local government meetings, collectively advocating for and ensuring the installation of street lights, construction of roads and provision of piped-clean water. One of them was elected as the panchayat president, with three others serving as ward members. This is a classic example of women leadership at the grassroots! Their position has ensured achieving a 100 per cent open defecation-free panchayat and support for the construction of a new school building.

HIH's training programmes have empowered these women with the confidence to bring about these changes at both personal and professional levels. Additionally, regular medical screening camps were conducted, specifically for non-communicable diseases, and it was also ensured that hot and healthy meals were provided at the *anganwadi* (children day care centres).

These pillars, over time, have evolved based on the needs of the people, the experience of the organization and the necessity to make the activities sustainable. Within five years of starting, I realized that relying solely on an NGO model would not be sustainable in the long run; I knew I had to balance this with for-profit entities. To address this, I acquired Belstar, a microfinance company, to cross-subsidize some of the costs of the pillars at HIH and ensure the sustainability of programmes like child labour elimination, which cannot even cover the salaries of employees.

∞

'The best way to predict the future is to invent it.'

—Alan Kay

Similar to Alan Kay, my vision has always been to imagine a bright, promising future by taking action to create it. It is easy to rest on our laurels, count our blessings and sit back, enjoying the sun. But it's a different ball game altogether to strive for quality work on a large scale to impact millions of lives.

My story is inspiring not because of what I achieved, but because of how it demonstrates the power of empathy for the less privileged, combined with a keen sense of business acumen and sheer professionalism.

The journey of HIH started with three people in a small house in South India who wanted to spread the importance of opportunity, consensus, collaboration, commitment and above all, character, which can resonate in any part of the world.

1

MY ROOTS

I was born into a typical South Indian middle-class family in Coimbatore and then raised in the coastal city of Chennai. Born after eight years of my parents' marriage, I was the eldest of three girls and welcomed with excitement and immense happiness. My parents, Dandapani and Vijayalakshmi, both worked for Indian government departments. They instilled in us the importance of values like hard work and honesty and prioritized our education so that we could become self-reliant and achieve our dreams.

My mother was an amiable and loving person, embodying limitless kindness, devotion and generosity. She was very courageous and maintained an excellent relationship with everyone with total equanimity. She was exceedingly bright and creative. My maternal grandfather was a railway contractor, exemplifying integrity, compassion and excellence in all his endeavours. He was my role model and I learnt tremendously from him.

My father was quite the opposite of my mother. He was

very strict and believed education to be of utmost importance, which should not be compromised at any cost. He set lofty goals for us. Though we lived in Pallavaram, a small area just near the Chennai Airport, he sent us to Fathima Convent—a school renowned for its quality education—all the way in Kodambakkam, which was a good 30-minute ride away. Similarly, I was enrolled in the prestigious Stella Maris College for an undergraduate degree in physics. Since he worked for the Indian Railways, he had a railway pass that we utilized every holiday. When I look back now, I fondly remember the train journeys we took across the country to Rishikesh, Kanyakumari, Delhi and Bombay as a family. His thirst for adventure and travel has surely been passed on to me as I love to visit new places and learn about different cultures even today.

My childhood was conventional yet endearing. We had the basic luxuries and a supportive environment that made it comfortable. I was not too studious but rather playful and mischievous. I caused enough trouble, prompting my father to enrol me in different schools. However, my notoriety was always balanced by my determination and innate curiosity to grow.

My younger sisters, Bindu and Kamini, were born nine and eleven years after me. Given the age difference, I became a maternal figure to them. They both are extremely bright and hardworking, shining through school and college. Bindu studied computer science, specializing in software and then working for big names like HCL, Amazon and currently, Coinbase. Kamini was the first to leave home for studies; she went to Coimbatore for her undergraduate engineering degree and then to the United States for her master's. She too has thrived in the competitive technology environment at California and is currently working for Airbnb. All three of us successfully balance our careers and families—a testament to our parents' value systems and upbringing. More than anything, our parents gave us the confidence and freedom of choice to learn and live life to our fullest potential.

∾

After I completed my graduation in physics, my marriage was fixed to Sankar, a civil servant whose job opened my eyes in many ways. In my generation, most parents felt that securing their daughters' marriage into a good family and investing in gold and property would be enough for her happiness. I also didn't know a lot about my spouse or his family before marriage as it was an arranged marriage. My in-laws were quite conservative and felt comfortable in only a traditional role for the woman of the house.

Initially, we moved around a lot due to my husband's transferable job. We started our life at Pollachi, a small town in Coimbatore, where my husband was the sub-collector. It was my first time running a household; we had little help but always loved hosting friends and family. Later we moved to another small town, Dharmapuri, before shifting to Chennai. Living in these small towns made me realize the importance of financial independence and a solid career. It was then that I decided to continue my education and pursue a career to fulfil my dreams. In the late 1980s, I pursued my master's degree through distance education.

The year 1992 was significant for us. We welcomed our daughter, Sahaana, and lady luck followed her arrival as my husband was transferred to Coimbatore—Tamil Nadu's second-largest district and referred to as the Manchester of southern India, as its collector. We lived there for two years.

Being the District Collector's family, we lived in a palatial house with more than a dozen servants, enjoying all the privileges entitled to a civil servant. We were engaged in most of the important events and celebrations. As the wife of a District Collector, I became an assigned leader of the Indian Red Cross Chapter and Women's Voluntary Service of the district. I had the opportunity to meet and host several famous personalities including the President, Vice President, Chief Minister and celebrities like Kapil Dev and so on. These experiences in Coimbatore nurtured my leadership skills as I handled the dignitaries, addressed the grievances of petitioners and solved problematic issues.

∽

During this period of being the collector's wife, a series of transformative episodes made me realize how material things and pleasures were temporary as circumstances could change overnight. My husband handled two sensitive assignments during his tenure. One was a law-and-order problem—a clash between Hindus and Muslims at Kottaimedu—a fallout stemming from the Babri Masjid demolition. The situation escalated to firing incidents, with the Muslims requesting my husband to enter their area unarmed amidst gunfire within a few metres. Even now when I pass through Kottaimedu, I am reminded of the incident and am thankful that my husband returned safely despite the ominous circumstances.

The second incident involved handling the dreaded sandalwood smuggler Veerappan. He had killed more than a hundred people, poached thousands of elephants and had his own fiefdom. He kidnapped three police officials from the district and demanded a hefty ransom of ₹1 billion to release them. This dreadful incident taught me the power of effective negotiation. My husband had to comfort the family members of the kidnapped officers, face relentless media scrutiny for a month, manage the police and take a just stand to pacify the smuggler. Threats against our daughter and me were common, with recorded cassettes arriving at our residence nightly, warning of dire consequences if my husband sided with the police. Veerappan was eventually killed in an encounter but the preceding days were terrifying; our phones were tapped and every move was monitored in the name of security.

Soon after this assignment, we moved back to Chennai where my husband continued to work in a plethora of government posts until his retirement as additional Chief Secretary of the Industries Department in 2016. In 1996, we spent a year in Australia while Sankar pursued his MBA from Southern Cross University. Watching Sahaana grow and learn English at Merle Rankin, a local playschool, remains fresh in my memory, as we bonded closely as a family.

By this time, I had already completed my Bachelor of Education and MSc in Physics. I enrolled for PhD in Theoretical Nuclear Physics at Madras University and started teaching physics to higher secondary students. I used to work on mainframe computers at the university and used my personal computer for equations and analysis. I navigated the challenging coursework alongside my classmates who were exceedingly bright and often from prestigious institutes like the Indian Institute of Technology (IIT), with the help of my guide, who was extremely helpful and helped me move in the right direction. I defended my thesis at the Presidency College, Madras, the alma mater of Nobel laureates Sir C.V. Raman and Dr Subramaniam Chandrasekhar. My external examiner was from the Los Alamos Lab in the USA, an institute known for its contribution to nuclear science. After seven years of hard work, I earned my PhD.

I also completed diplomas in Information Technology from the National Institute of Information Technology and Management Information Systems from the Southern Cross University.

&

Even today, whenever I talk about my education, people are amazed at how I could complete this tough journey while being married and balancing motherhood. I must give credit to my father for instilling in all of us the drive to keep improving ourselves. He constantly sought better assignments to provide for us, even opting to work in Algeria, staying alone and saving money for his daughters' dreams. His vision and hard work paid off, with all the three of us excelling in our professions. Credit also goes to my husband for being ever so accommodating and understanding. He valued my opinions and gave importance to my aspirations as much as his own. He was always available for Sahaana when I had to travel for work or education. He used to participate in household responsibilities equally—a key driver for women's careers to thrive post marriage and motherhood.

Sankar has been my bouncing board to date, providing me with invaluable guidance and perspective from his own field experiences across the country. His feedback has shaped my thought process and decision-making. He has always been exceptionally kind and treats everyone equally—be it a personal assistant, a driver or the chief minister. He is the sort of person who would go to any extent to help someone in need, especially his friends. This sort of kindness leaves an impression and has moulded my character and approach towards people.

Raising my daughter Sahaana has been a pleasure. She was never a troublesome child and always very well behaved. Watching her grow from a toddler who never uttered an English word to one who graduated from the London School of Economics (LSE) has been an exciting experience. After a certain age, daughters become their mother's best friend and this was the case for us too. She joined me at HIH in 2015 after her graduation and has been integral in communicating my work to the external stakeholders. My professional travels with her have been very special as we are able to bond, and she gets a first-hand view and understanding of the rationale behind every decision I make. She has been critical in bringing in new trends and technology to HIH. Even after her marriage in 2016 to Srashta, she has continued to support HIH and curving her path as a leader in her own unique style. My most recent role, and most important, is that of a grandmother to two-year-old Samaira, my granddaughter in whom I see glimpses of myself.

My personal and professional lives have always been intertwined as I have valued Sankar's inputs at every step of the way and now Sahaana helps me with consolidating my work.

I remember joining the Cancer Institute in Chennai under Dr Shanta to pursue a career in what I had studied for. I quit on day one as I couldn't stomach the immense suffering of cancer patients. This may seem like a lack of courage to continue but I see it as a brave step to change my career path. Transitioning from my specialization to a government job dealing with gender, grassroots women and policy, without any background in it, was a new terrain but a challenge I took up and thrived in.

Shifting from a stable government job to running a fledgling NGO too was a risk but one that has led me to where I am today. My roots have given me the strength to handle the several challenges at HIH and Belstar. I wouldn't have it any other way!

2

THE BEGINNING

28 MARCH 2004

I was on my way to Kanchipuram from Chennai to be interviewed for a new organization called Hand in Hand.

I had very little idea about the background and operations of the organization except that it was a non-profit organization run by two Swedish teachers, Olle and Gunnel Blomqvist. They came to India and started HIH in Kanchipuram, Tamil Nadu, in 2000, primarily to take up education activities for poor children, especially from tribal families and those trapped in child labour.

I was going to be interviewed by an industrialist from Sweden named Percy Barnevik. With an engineering degree from Stanford University, he started his career at Sandvik before making a name for himself due to his role in the formation of Asea Brown Boveri (ABB) through the merger of Sweden's Allmanna Svenska Elektriska Aktiebolaget (ASEA) and Switzerland's Brown, Boveri & Cie. He rose to be the chairman of ABB and later the pharmaceutical giant, AstraZeneca. Barnevik also served on the boards of several multinational companies, including General Motors of USA and DuPont. As an acknowledged expert on strategic globalization and the management of big enterprises, he had an extensive network of connections in both corporate and political circles worldwide. My husband, Sankar, who had read about him in the very first chapter of his Strategic Management course during his MBA, couldn't believe that Percy was going to interview me!

I had been working as the Monitoring and Evaluation officer in Tamil Nadu Corporation for Development of Women for 10 years. My job was to finalize a Poverty Reduction and Empowerment Project to be funded by the World Bank. My decade-long tenure had provided me considerable experience in the formation and management of women's SHGs by working closely with hundreds of NGOs as this concept was gaining popularity in Tamil Nadu back then. I also learnt about the different models of SHGs and the best practices from other states such as Andhra Pradesh, Madhya Pradesh and Kerala.

I felt that my current job was only partly utilizing my expertise and the new assignment with HIH promised to be better.

❧

With donations from other Swedish teachers and acquaintances, Olle and Gunnel Blomqvist started a small school, a few crèches called *daghis*, some evening tuition centres and transit schools for dropout children and a few tailoring training centres. They also launched a nutrition scheme to help poor families with provisions needed for a month and attempted to build houses for the tribal families in a village.

Upon learning of these activities, Percy Barnevik took a trip to India in late 2003 and recognized the potential for an even greater impact. The only factor missing was solid leadership—someone with impeccable management skills and a deep understanding of the Indian social milieu and dynamics.

As was his style, Percy created a detailed note on what could be achieved with a new team in place. Having been a regular visitor to India since the late 1960s, he had a fairly accurate view of both India's potential and the bottlenecks holding the country back. He could see that while China was growing very fast, with a focussed and strategic vision, India lagged by a few decades in every aspect despite holding great promise.

During his initial pitch presentations to the donor community, Barnevik drew comparisons between the two countries based on his knowledge as he had investments in India and China. He emphasized how China was ahead in terms of demographics, literacy rates, infrastructure, governance and labour market flexibility. Given his involvement in advising governments and corporates on these critical issues, he came across Tarun Das, the Secretary-General of the Confederation of Indian Industry (CII) during one of the high-level conferences he had attended. Barnevik requested Das' help in identifying a competent leader with the right aptitude for managing HIH. The CII Chennai office was already aware of my credentials and recommended me for an interview with Percy, along with a few others.

❧

Emma House, the headquarters for the NGO, was a small two-storey rented house in Kanchipuram. I was a bit taken aback upon reaching the venue. The office space was at the end of a dark and eerie corridor and was used both as a living and dining room. The interview lasted two hours and Percy, who had a knack for shortlisting talents across diverse cultures and skill sets for global enterprises, immediately recognized my potential.

My qualifications and experience appeared to align perfectly with the needs of the fledgling NGO. His only concern was the support I could expect from my family to devote my full attention to the job which would require me to travel from my home 70 km away.

Despite the stability and opportunities that came with a government job, I was excited to work at the grassroots level to understand the plight and grievances of marginalized communities and alleviate them to the best of my capacity. I was ready to take a leap of faith and explore an uncharted territory. I decided to take a few years' leave to test the waters and see how it all worked out.

Thus began this incredible journey for both Percy and I—starkly different personalities from two different parts of the world coming together for a joint mission.

3

THE INITIAL STRUGGLES

When you think of international not-for-profit organizations, you might imagine a well-funded balance sheet, plush offices and highly qualified staff. You would expect key stakeholders to bring in partnerships and an array of opportunities waiting to be tapped into. When I joined HIH, I was confronted with the polar opposite!

Going through the accounts of HIH (Sweden–Tamil Nadu) for the year 2002–03, the year before I joined, I found that in the absence of all the details of payments and vouchers, the accountant had prepared a bare minimum balance sheet totalling a princely amount of ₹1,75,000 with a cash balance of just ₹3,048.[1]

HIH ran several initiatives such as the Olle Primary School, a tailoring project, a transit school, a separate school for tribal children, a few daghis, a programme that provided food items to about 110 children and an evening school for the children of weavers who had dropped out of school, with a total annual budget of the amount of ₹1,75,000.[2] The trust engaged about 25 part-time workers to run these programmes at relatively low salaries ranging between ₹300–1,000 per month.

I had to start from scratch to streamline the whole organization, which was content to run these initiatives with minimal staff and very low overall costs. While I was more than willing to give it my all, I hoped to have a better support system to carry out the challenging task at hand.

I started from the top—when I joined, the trust had three local staff members who were being paid monthly salaries and attended to the needs of the donors and the programmes in a limited way. Percy and other foreign donors wanted to see some significant change, both in the field and the organization, but my onboarding as the chief executive officer (CEO) was met with a lot of resistance.

Coming from a background of pure science and nuclear physics, my approach to problem-solving was scientific. I was keen on identifying the root cause of problems and resolving them systematically. My ideology for not-for-profit work was that we should be present 24×7 for any support or resolution of issues, with all data captured for impact-oriented long-term solutions. Coming from Chennai and not being a local didn't bode well in my favour. Additionally, being a female added to it as most of the staff refused to report to me.

I used to travel two hours on a rickety road from Chennai to Kanchipuram each morning, only to be greeted with unwelcoming smiles and unbending attitudes. There was no willingness to share any information, which made my tasks extremely difficult to execute. Prior to my joining, the staff enjoyed freedom in terms of spending and implementing programmes at random, with no plan or focus. The organization had been functioning since 1998 and by 2004, not one student had passed grade 10! Accounts were almost non-existent, with many of the assets being bought in the names of individuals and not the trust. The school's income was never brought into account and was simply pocketed. There was practically no interaction with the local government. I insisted on proper invoicing and transparency, which was not appreciated.

I began to finalize the accounts for the year that ended March 2004 with the available records and bank statements and arrived at this conclusion:

Income = ₹9,00,000

Expenditure = ₹7,85,000[3]

I introduced standard procedures for accounts and programme expenditures with clear processes for approvals and implementation. All the assets were brought into account wherever possible with the available records but I also realized that many would never be brought into account. The limitations of the local leadership and lack of experience and exposure could have been the reasons for this disorganized structure. To overcome this, I hired an accountant from Chennai and used his support to track the accounts. I also spent time networking and revamping the board with people of repute and importance to not only bring value to our operations but also guide on good governance practices. For instance, for the schools, I brought in a senior educationist with a passion for Montessori education to revise the curriculum and update the teaching methodology. To formalize the school, I applied for recognition from the Education Department. I spent time visiting the Collectorate and establishing a rapport with the district administration to ensure their support while implementing projects at the grassroots.

I knew that I had to build a cohort of qualified staff who would act with conscience, passion and information to build a credible organization.

I relied on the learnings from my previous work experience with the government to strengthen leadership at the senior and grassroots levels at HIH India in the early days. I used my contacts at institutions such as Mysore Resettlement and Development Agency (MYRADA) and other reputed NGOs in India to reach out to staff who would be willing to shift their base to Kanchipuram. Nearly 20 staff migrated from MYRADA as the funding for a project was concluding and their contracts were ending. Each of these staff brought immense experience in the middle level and helped boost our local presence. At the top level, I met with government officials and hired women from reputed families to lead the team in letter and spirit. We had volunteers and senior consultants from Sweden to help us in setting up communications, branding and donor relations. These struggles in the early days helped me build a strong base of staff, some of whom are still with us 20 years later!

෴

I was tasked with tackling the rampant child labour in the silk weaving looms after my joining. Every day, I would hear gloomy stories of children trapped in labour and debt bondage that kept me up at night.

I was particularly shaken by the story of a painter who had lost his wife. As a result of abject poverty, he had to sell his child off for less than a paltry sum of just ₹500 as a bonded labourer.[4] The boy was barely five years old. I still remember the innocent look in his eyes, which pierced my heart when I met him.

With support from an early staff member, Rex Vazz, who was then working on child labour elimination initiatives, we enrolled the boy in a residential school, after which he was mainstreamed to a government school and is now living a dignified and happy life.

We faced a lot of resistance while working to free children from labour and bondage. In this particular case, the father cooperated and all we needed was some funding to ensure the boy didn't drop out of school. I still remember handing over a suitcase from my home to him to carry his things to school!

One incident that lingers in my memory is of Kanakaraj, who hails from Kangeyam in Thiruppur district, Tamil Nadu. When he first told me about his life as a child labour, I was shocked. The family used to earn ₹300 per day for breaking 1,000 coconuts. As an adult I can barely break one and it was unimaginable for me that a child with nimble fingers and petite palms had to break 100. Machinery was fast replacing these child labourers but Kanakaraj's family didn't want that as his income was essential for the family to make their ends meet. My team and I enrolled Kanakaraj into a local school and supported him till he passed grade 10. He currently works as driver in Krishnagiri, earning a decent living.

HIH had acquired land to build a residential school for dropouts but no buildings were in sight. My first task was to identify a good construction agency. My previous job had involved meeting a lot of non-governmental agencies who were keen on partnering with the government in its many livelihood programmes.

One of them had expertise on low-cost technology popularized by one Mr Laurie Baker, who built cost-effective structures using locally available materials. The first residential school of HIH at Putheri near Kanchipuram, called Poongavanam (forest of flowers) was constructed in record time. We inaugurated it in exactly six months after my joining. The school could accommodate about 100 children and had 51 children at the end of the year.

Poongavanam went on to be one of HIH India's landmark initiatives, housing close to 1,000 children to date. The project has been supported by the Sarva Shiksha Abhiyan (now Samagrah Siksha) of Governments of India and Tamil Nadu and other generous individuals and corporates, making it a model institution.

The child-centric programmes were brought under an umbrella programme titled the Child Labour Elimination Project (CLEP), which was felicitated with the 'Bal Kalyan Puraskar' by the President of India in 2019. The non-negotiables for this project were that every child must attend full-time formal day school and any child out of school was to be considered a child labourer.

I partnered with MVF, which also followed similar non-negotiables for their child labour elimination initiatives and were very firm on not adopting short-term measures like paying off the loan money to the employer of the child labourer to free the child from the bond. Their approach involved organizing village-level rallies to sensitize all the parents to send their children to formal schools. The MVF volunteers had a full repertoire of such rallies, street plays, songs and one-to-one meetings with whoever could support their cause. They were relentless and single-minded in their conviction that there has to be a gradual but firm change in the mindset of the people to make these programmes successful. They roped in the local body leaders like the village panchayat presidents, school teachers, and even women and the children themselves.

My team and the volunteers of MVF were mocked routinely and faced physical abuse in some areas where child labour was an essential part of the economy. The project provided invaluable insight to me and my team on the essentials of a grassroots-level programme, giving them a permanent place in the villages they worked in. We realized that these impoverished families lacked access to information and the tangible benefits of education. Their primary focus was to earn a basic sum every day to put a square meal on the table and not go hungry. This was their everyday problem and thinking long-term could not be a part of their plan as their life revolved around tough manual labour that stretched long hours, with them often returning home to domestic quarrels. It was usually the elder siblings who looked after the young ones and not the parents. The families were broken with each one having to fend for themselves. Any additional income was a bonus.

On close interaction, we traced the most influential touch points in the village. In some cases, it was the elderly, in others it was the youth and some others, retired headmasters. Each of these groups understood the value of education and how it could be the only tool that may bring out the families from poverty. We used them to propagate the message of right to education!

The first annual report of HIH, which I got printed, had the following words on the back cover in addition to the non-negotiables of the CLEP:

'Any justification perpetuating the existence of child labour must be condemned.'

The organization firmly ignored arguments about the 'harsh reality' of the family, poverty, the necessity of the child's earning for the family, lack of interest among the parents, poor quality of teachers, the irrelevance of education in providing employment and so on, considering all these as anti-children and detrimental to their real development.

As in everything else, I made the best efforts to make the residential school a model besides the cost-effective buildings. I visited Isai Ambalam, which means 'Temple of Music', a school that emphasizes the joy of learning, at the international community of Auroville, Puducherry, about 100 km from Chennai. This school adopted a ladder approach[5] to teaching the basics of every subject, kindling the fascination of the child with new ideas and concepts and laying stress only on the joy of learning. It allowed children to progress at their own pace, internalizing the learning gradually but permanently.

For HIH under my leadership, the child-centric approach was not merely a slogan; it was initiated, nurtured, sustained and breathed life into each and every activity. Under this approach, we focussed on the child holistically—not stopping with education but including mental and physical health. The children led the way on the path they wanted to take while the teachers and our team acted as catalysts to help them achieve their goals.

As Percy Barnevik used to say often, we decided not to give up on any child whatever the circumstances.

∞

In the first year we enrolled 131 children, but 80 left midway, citing all kinds of vague reasons, like a grandmother's severe illness, which were beyond my comprehension. It took me some time to realize that simply providing a regular environment for studying was not enough for children who had dropped out or had never been enrolled in school. These families and children had never seen successful role models in their immediate environment who had succeeded purely through education. A lot more needed to be done to win over these families.

The residential schools were what we had envisioned—a nurturing homely environment. We provided nutritious food, a safe place to stay and lots of care. The full-time Residential Special Training Centre (RSTC) model meant that students, teachers and support staff were present 365 days, 24×7, relentless and passionate in their commitment. Some of the teachers went above and beyond their duties, teaching 10-year-old children to brush their teeth, comb their hair and wash their clothes. Sometimes they had to search the entire town for absconding students and stay up all night when they were sick with fever or other health issues—providing the students with all these facilities convinced donors and the government of the authenticity and success of our model.

In the early days, all our endeavours were viewed very differently from the students' eyes. They were grateful but they were also demanding in their own way. During one of my early visits, one young boy screamed at me that the food and menu weren't to his liking! I was taken aback as we were doing everything possible for their education and safety. But then, we tried putting ourselves in their shoes and expanded the menu, focussed on mental health and ensured they could enjoy their lost childhood before diving into education. Later, this boy moved to the Adi Dravida Welfare hostel at Walajabad and topped his class 10th examination. The students and teachers at the RSTC reiterated the fact that we could mould children's future with love, affection and care!

~

At the end of the first year, HIH under my leadership had mainstreamed about 1,200 children, including about 50 bonded labourer children, into about 150 government schools through a series of rallies, meetings and door-to-door canvassing. The evening schools, which were initially for children who weaved during the day, were phased out as the objective was to bring the children to fully formal day schools. They were replaced with transit schools for the children who had failed in a few subjects to cross over public exams in classes 8th, 10th and 12th.

A very significant step was the establishment of a full-fledged residential school, which followed the ladder pedagogical methodology to keep the children motivated and free from fears of learning difficulties.

As part of its advocacy efforts, HIH also got an order issued by the Government of Tamil Nadu, permitting government schools to admit the students who were either dropouts or who had not been enrolled in schools previously as they were mainstreamed by organizations like HIH throughout the year instead of only up to September. This change prevented many children from returning to work simply because they couldn't enrol until the next academic year.

My first six months at HIH went by in a flicker. Despite the challenges of commute, acceptance, funding and finding the right talent, I could already see the tangible benefits of my work on the ground. HIH's service to the community reminded me of the impact that influential leaders like

Mahatma Gandhi had made on society. I realized the power of education and community service. The insights from the CLEP made me think deeply about the multidimensional aspects of poverty that needed to be addressed.

I was just starting and there was no looking back!

4

TACKLING MULTIDIMENSIONAL POVERTY

I had been working on developing the CLEP for HIH for close to six months. Our first RSTC was open, with children breathing life into the walls, but many more children still remained out of school.

While poverty was undoubtedly the root cause, I knew that our problem ran much deeper. Through several interactions with the children and their families and analysing the reasons for the children being sent for work, I realized that household income levels were extremely low for assetless families. There was no way for a permanent solution unless such endemic poverty was tackled effectively through loan and saving schemes.

I had extensive experience in the formation and successful running of women's SHGs in my earlier job. Many of them were coming out of the poverty trap by building their small-scale enterprises. Women needed to be empowered financially as it would not only add to their family's incomes but also allow them to send their children to school.

∞

The SHG movement had manifested itself in many forms through poverty alleviation programmes primarily funded by the Government of India. It started with the Integrated Rural Development Programme, or IRDP as it was famously referred to, which funded millions of goats, sheep and milch cattle throughout India for many years. An insurance brass tag was pierced into the ear lobes of the animals, resulting in the rural areas being filled with ear-torn cattle owing to the massive recycling of the same animals under the programme. No wonder the programme needed a drastic overhaul!

One of the ideas that emerged was the concept of group lending where groups stood as guarantees for the repayment of all the loans taken by their members. Pioneering work conducted under an International Fund for Agricultural Development (IFAD) project in some of the districts of Tamil Nadu with the help of NGOs like the MYRADA, demonstrated the potential of women's SHGs as harbingers of a path-breaking movement to eradicate rural poverty. Women proved to be reliable borrowers as they started saving from day one. They were also enterprising and worked well within a group setting. Banks found them more amenable to being disciplined and were willing to commit large funds to finance them.

On a particular field visit to Trichy during my days at Women's Development Corporation, I came across an old woman who had taken a loan of ₹3,000 for selling betel leaves and nuts. I saw her running the enterprise independently and found her ability to repay ₹100 every day with the sales she was making while keeping a profit remarkable.

Entrepreneurship was the key to poverty alleviation and I just knew that we had to include this as a pillar of HIH's work.

To tackle poverty by using entrepreneurship as a weapon, I launched women's SHGs by combining the joint liability concept piloted by Nobel Peace Prize laureate Mr Mohammed Yunus[1] in Bangladesh and the savings culture promoted by the IFAD project.[2] The SHGs typically consist of 10–15 women from similar socioeconomic backgrounds in the same village with its success stemming from women gaining solidarity and strength in a group setting. On 1 September 2004, HIH disbursed its first loans to these SHGs, aiming to create a million jobs envisioned by Percy Barnevik and me. He was sold on the concept of creating enterprises with small loans but the speed at which I started the initiative surprised him. Securing a loan was not easy. I took a loan from the Indian Bank, Theradi Branch, in Kanchipuram to lend to SHGs. I had to provide a personal guarantee for this pilot initiative as it was not part of the budget.

HIH's model had some unique features—groups of women with common interests were carefully chosen and provided orientation training on the group's activities. While the Grameen Model of Mr Yunus emphasized small loans for microenterprises and the joint liability of each member for the repayment of the loans, the HIH model strived for a 'credit plus' model, integrating savings and other activities like health, nutrition, insurance and capacity building. To empower these women in every possible way, one of the early interventions was to start a literacy programme, enabling these mostly illiterate women to gain functional literacy, simple numeracy skills for calculations and basic accounting knowledge.

The SHGs enabled most of these women to have bank accounts in their names for the first time in their lives. Group dynamics and social cohesion of the groups were observed for at least six months and the women were taught to conduct group meetings, save and lend among themselves. HIH motivated these women to become self-reliant rather than solely depend on HIH for their needs, encouraging the women to take loans from banks at lower interest rates, unlike the other microlending institutions in the field.

I truly believed that the real empowerment of women was not possible without all these measures, which reduced their vulnerabilities to the maximum possible extent and enhanced their participation in increasing the income of the family.

As I mentioned in my report to the Board of Directors in April 2005,[3] almost a year after my joining, HIH's strengths in the SHG intervention were the selection of relevant projects, close monitoring and robust targeting methodology. The second pillar in the HIH story was firmly in place.

∞

Building the SHG pillar with high-quality groups was not an easy task. In the early days, I would form SHGs by motivating the women in the morning, only to have other NGOs dissolve them by evening, citing HIH's lack of government affiliation. But I did not give up that easily. I would be back the next morning, pursuing them for just one opportunity to make a difference in their lives.

For the very first SHG bank linkage, I distinctly remember visiting the bank 20 times. The rural welfare officer affiliated to the bank, Mr Sukumar, left his home at 4 a.m. I used to set an alarm so that I could wake up early and follow him to work to get his help in securing the bank linkage. After looking at my perseverance and hearing me out, he understood my struggles and finally introduced me to the bank manager. The lead district manager, Mr Swaminathan, was also very receptive and took my case forward, which really boosted my morale.

~

The breakthrough in this SHG initiative was when the first SHG that I mentored set up their own enterprise—Crisp Bakery. These women were adept at making pickles and pappadams at home and wanted to expand their business.

By helping them start the bakery, I felt my own entrepreneurial journey taking off. I learnt about dough and temperature and the importance of the right packing material to keep buns soft. My colleague, Dr Madhu Sharan, and I went to Parry's Corner in Chennai to buy packing material in bulk for the women. We facilitated their first big order of supplying 1,000 buns and biscuits during tea time to Intimate Fashions, a large manufacturer in Sriperumbudur. We provided additional loans for a transport vehicle and to expand their machinery. We guided them to take an annual maintenance contract for all the equipment.

Crisp Bakery, under the leadership of Sheela, won the 'Best SHG Award' from Indian Bank. The award was presented by the former President of India Shri Abdul Kalam in 2006. Sheela became a successful entrepreneur, employing six other women in her bakery, and also the proud mother of an engineer and a doctor. This is the power of women entrepreneurship.

*

The end of the first year of the SHG pillar in 2005, saw the formation of 520 women's SHGs with 9,600 members involved in 60 trades with loan assistance of the first million rupees from the funds of HIH, along with savings of half a million rupees from the members' own funds. The women could not believe that their collective savings could be so substantial and that they were becoming an economic power all by themselves so quickly. The repayment rate was a neat 100 per cent![4]

Encouraged by the success of these enterprises, I brought out a compendium of 50 project proposals for microenterprises, in collaboration with the Tamil Nadu Small and Tiny Industries Association–Friedrich Naumann Stiftung Foundation (TANSTIA-FNF) Service Centre at Chennai. This compendium detailed the production process, working capital and investment needs, marketing and managing the enterprise so that first-time entrepreneurs could straightaway approach financial institutions with bankable projects.

*

HIH was already running a few tailoring centres for training women and using the machines for local jobs.

Within three months of my joining, I started a modern tailoring unit with power machines in the name of Aina Barnevik, Percy's wife, with an initial investment of just ₹2,75,000. To meet the demands of the growing garment industry, we designed a rigorous one-month training programme for unemployed rural female youth, charging a minimum fee of ₹50 at the time of admission. An agreement was facilitated with local garment factories such as Intimate Fashions and Celebrity Fashions for absorbing these trained women at fair wages and providing transportation and food. More than 130 women were trained in a six-month period with most securing jobs in the garment units.

Initially, the attrition rates were close to 50 per cent as these young women were unable to cope with the high standardization requirements of the structured garment industry. To address this, we included soft skills training, counselling the women and their parents on the nature of the job and emphasized the importance of hydration along with nutritious food to cope with standing and pedalling for close to eight hours.

In South India, it is common for women to use turmeric, both as a facial cleanser and for cooking. The potent remnants of this spice left yellow stains on the delicate garments. We sensitized the women on these cultural components as well. We created a small alumni group of trained women to counsel and mentor the younger lot. All these factors led to a rapid increase in retention rates. The corporates preferred HIH-trained women, making this model a real success!

To ensure the sustainability of the tailoring centre, we started retaining some women as a part of a small production centre within the same campus. These women were often single or older in age and couldn't cope with the demands of the factories but had adequate skills to stitch shirts and salwars, which they sold through the centre, generating income for themselves and making the unit self-sustainable.

The year 2005 also saw the establishment of the first Village Resource Centre (which later evolved into the Citizens' Centre) in March. The concept behind this centre was to provide a one-stop information cum service hub for the village, operated on public premises. The centre would have volunteers to assist the villagers in accessing all the government programmes and help in writing applications for various services. It would have a library, a fax or copier machine and a computer for data processing and training purposes.

As was done with the other pillars, I sought the help of Catalyst Trust, an NGO, to provide the basics of this centre. As the Right to Information Act was to be passed in the same year by the Government of India, HIH positioned itself directly to disseminate information, which would complement its efforts in developing women entrepreneurs and future leaders. The tangible results were evident as people could access their documents, board results and other essential items easily in one place. Dalits and the marginalized were able to retrieve their *patta* (land) documents with ease. Admission to colleges also became simpler and these outcomes aligned with our child labour elimination pillar.

❧

In my first year at HIH, I initiated several initiatives such as the CLEP, the SHG programme that provided microcredit to women and the Citizens' Centre project for information dissemination and good governance initiatives. While a small-scale health initiative involving children was already in place, I was determined to expand it as the fourth pillar of HIH's work by conducting health camps and supporting health and nutrition-related work.

The main reason for starting a health initiative stemmed from my extensive fieldwork with women at the bottom of the pyramid. I vividly remember an encounter with a woman affected by chikungunya at Thiruvallur. She had taken a microfinance loan from us to run her enterprise but was struggling to repay it and support her family due to prolonged illness and poor access to medical facilities.

I noticed how poor people neglected their health and had to rush to hospitals that are often hundreds of kilometres away from their villages. HIH started upgrading and improving the anganwadis in India as part of the health initiative. Additionally, we established single-doctor medical clinics to serve remote villages that had no medical care facilities. Observing gaps in the government healthcare system, we sought to fill them by partnering with them, ensuring continued access to healthcare for rural communities.

In the mid-2000s, we hosted several international visitors and delegations who came to see our projects in the field. Even though they were fascinated by our culture and traditions, they always commented on the poor upkeep of our cities and public areas. They used to tell me, 'Kalpana, you do such impactful work in uplifting women and putting children back in school; why can't you take up the issue of waste management?'

~

In 2008, I forayed into the area of solid waste management in a small way in Mudichur, Tamil Nadu. We appointed Green Friends, who were basically sanitary workers, in several villages and worked closely with the local governments to provide a clean environment in a sustainable way. Our approach involved implementing user charges (charging the user for proper disposal and segregation of waste to ensure a sense of commitment to the cause), source segregation (of waste as biodegradable, non-biodegradable and inert), recycling and reuse. We first tried working with rag pickers but their entire process was not organized and it did not solve the problem of reducing waste that ends at landfill. So instead, we came up with the concept of 'Green Friends'. I ensured that they were mostly women who needed a new lease of life. By giving them gloves, coats, caps and enough training on the importance of segregation of waste at source, I created a sense of dignity and pride associated with their work. To instil further security, we arranged for Employees' State Insurance, provident funds (PFs) and health insurance for them. I also arranged for a visit to Sweden for the team to understand the best practices in waste management that we could replicate in India.

The environment pillar then grew from just waste management to include Water and soil conservation works with the support of the National Bank for Agriculture and Rural Development (NABARD).

❧

A massive tsunami struck Tamil Nadu in December 2004, claiming the lives of almost 8,000 people and affecting the livelihoods of thousands of families settled along the coastal belt.

This incident was another pivotal moment in my first year at HIH as I learnt that the community development sector could never work with a fixed blueprint or business plan. We have to respond to the needs of the people as and when required, in as structured a way as possible. Due to the tsunami, people in the coastal regions near Villupuram district lost their homes, belongings and livelihoods. Through a partner NGO, HIH contributed to rescuing people from this mammoth natural disaster by distributing food, clothing, fishnets and boats and helped many children with notebooks and other materials to tide them over the immediate distress. My philosophy then (and now) is to never reject any opportunity to help people. Even ₹100 can go a long way to make a difference and create goodwill in society.

The year had been one of tremendous growth and expansion for HIH. As Percy noted in his report to the HIH Sweden board in April 2005, the organization had grown from about 25 full-time employees to about 150, with 50 of them having college degrees. The activities consolidated the existing projects with fresh initiatives in new areas of operation, the most notable being the women's SHGs.

Percy noted that the team and I had achieved extraordinary expansion with the retention of good quality (many projects with almost no credit losses) and with good control over all the activities, especially in expenditure and accounting for the same. He was happy to see that this expansion was done along with the weeding out of dishonesty from the system and the establishment of good protocols for the processes.

From an annual expenditure of about ₹1,75,000 and a cash balance of just ₹3,048 in the year before, the balance sheet after the first year under my management had grown to about ₹7.5 million and a cash balance of almost ₹3 million.[5]

In fact, for the first time, the Swedish donors and the Board got full-fledged accounts with all the investments and expenditures neatly presented after an auditor had certified the same. I also followed up on getting the necessary approvals from the Government of India for their own foreign remittance account.

Aside from strategizing for implementation, I worked on strengthening governance aspects in the first year. I got renowned professionals from the private and NGO sectors to assist me as the Board of Trustees to enable me maintain high standards from the first day. The first was Dr Mangala Ayre, an educationist who moved from Chennai to Kanchipuram to assist us with running the schools. She has been steadfast in her support and is always available locally. Her unique ability to develop pre-kindergarten syllabi for students and teacher training set our school apart and has been attracting hundreds of new students to date.

Mr Venkat Reddy of MVF helped lay the fundamental principles for eradicating child labour and his work left a deep impression on me. Later on, Dr Sudarshan, a Padma awardee, joined us. Mr Reddy and Dr Sudarshan have dedicated their entire life to the sake of children and child rights, and providing better health facilities to remote communities, respectively. From them, I learnt the strong values of humility, patience and commitment—values I carry with me to date every day.

Mr Kottaisamy, Mr K.N. Krishnamurthy and Mr N. Srinivasan had invaluable experience in the development and corporate sectors, which helped in adding a professional flavour to our operations including human resources, trends in the development sector, aligning with government policies and providing a corporate outlook.

Prof. Arun Kumar of IIT Madras, as a Trustee, brought in an academic perspective, leveraging his expertise in management studies to benefit our graduated women entrepreneurs. Chandrasekar and Raghu, both chartered accountants, have been extremely supportive of our initiatives over the past several years. Amuthasekaran has been part of the HIH journey since the early days. Mr M.S. Sundararajan, former chief managing director of Indian Bank has been a steadfast supporter as an adviser. He gave me strength during difficult times and steered the Board forward in the right direction with the highest accounting and finance standards.

I owe a lot to this Board with rich experience in audit, finance and the development sector who guided me to develop programmes tuned to the Indian context.

All these milestones appear to have been easily achieved now after so many years but I had to face tremendous hurdles due to my insistence on setting right the organization and its procedures. People used to buy assets in their own name instead of the institutions. They could not adjust to the rightful registration of these assets in the name of HIH India as they got used to the freedom of being direct beneficiaries of the asset holding.

Rival organizations could not stomach the rapid expansion as HIH's growth could threaten their own existence and started writing endless petitions to all the officials making wild allegations. Nothing would come out of such assertions but I had to spend time and energy repeatedly answering such complaints. I had to recruit new qualified people from scratch to expedite the growth of the organization.

The NGO sector was not the first choice as an employment option for many qualified people especially as the work was in Kanchipuram, about 70 km from Chennai. I had to travel daily from my residence in Chennai, which added to the exertion, but I was clear that I had to be physically present and get my hands dirty to achieve HIH's mission.

Apart from integrity, my employees had to display professional expertise and commitment. It was also necessary to pay at least the market-level salaries, but this entailed extra cost.

I also insisted that staff at all levels be given PFs, employee insurance and other benefits as per the government mandate. With the main thrust on eradication of child and bonded labour and poverty alleviation, the NGO had to show that it was a model employer too.

The NGO sector was generally perceived as one for the truly committed but underpaid employees who could work on shoestring budgets. Bringing in a culture of high-quality performance to work for the poor and marginalized was a big challenge I faced, but this was required to set HIH firmly on its path-breaking journey.

The year was spent on building a strong foundation in terms of quality in implementation standards, getting the right human resources, revamping the Board, laying the standard processes that would inform the way forward for the initiatives to be taken by the organization and establishing relationships with multiple stakeholders in the areas HIH was working.

In 2005, Percy and I were already thinking of taking this model all over the world starting with South Africa and Afghanistan. Percy was an advisory council member for the South African government. Through this, he knew Nelson Mandela and President Thabo Mbeki and briefed them about our project in India. Similarly, in Afghanistan, Percy knew President Hamid Karzai, whom he had previously met in London. With support from India's Ministry of External Affairs, we could launch our pilot there. Thus the HIH model was on the cusp of global replication!

5

THE GLOBAL FOOTPRINTS

'If you light a lamp for someone else,
it will also brighten up your path.'

—Gautama Buddha

Percy's vision of taking the HIH model globally began taking shape as early as 2005. By 2007, HIH India was working across 72 districts in India, covering three states (Tamil Nadu, Karnataka and Madhya Pradesh) and one union territory (Puducherry).

The 25-member staff expanded into 5,600 full-time employees and about 1,400 part-time and full-time consultants, totalling a neat 7,000 professionals.[1] The speed with which I had set up the first 520 women's SHGs convinced Percy that this strategy would be ideal for a global programme to eradicate poverty and achieve other objectives on health, child mortality, illiteracy and optimizing the standard of living.[2]

While on a visit to South Africa to attend the funeral of Nelson Mandela's son, Makgatho Mandela, Percy had a long chat with Mr Mandela, informing him about the rapid scale-up of microenterprises created by HIH and how a similar programme could help South Africa. He was a member of the International Investment Council (IIC), which Mr Mandela had formed in 1999 to facilitate the flow of investments into South Africa. Percy also discussed replicating the successfully piloted model from India with the President of South Africa, Thabo Mbeki.

In 2005, a five-member team had come for a G20 meeting from South Africa to India, led by the Minister for Agriculture and Land Affairs, Thoko Didiza. On 19 March 2005, they visited Kanchipuram and interacted with a number of women's SHGs assisted by HIH.

The minister wanted to know how the poor could be given resources without any subsidy as South Africa had a policy of not offering subsidies since the late 1990s. There was hardly any private sector funding available for the rural poor. There was practically no involvement of the people in poverty alleviation or rural development programmes. They were impressed by the rotation of the savings among the groups and the adoption of best practices from both the Grameen Model and the SHG model. This approach was successful due to the spreading of risk and the excellent repayment rates by the women.

Thus began a path breaking story of South-South Cooperation (SSC)[3] between India and South Africa.

❧

My first trip to South Africa was in mid-2005. I had only read about and seen its beauty and culture in a plethora of National Geographic shows. I travelled on South African

Airways, which had a stopover in Dubai. The journey was long and tiring, as expected. Not anticipating the stress of a long flight and time difference, as was my style, I packed my trip with meetings and visits so I could get back home as soon as possible to be with my family.

Upon landing, Madhu Sharan, the then-project director for the SHG programme, and I immediately went for a field visit that lasted almost the entire day. We had a meeting with the First Lady for dinner, which I missed because I was exhausted from the journey.

This was my first learning—while travelling abroad, always go a day earlier to acclimatize to the changing environment and try to travel in the business class for longer trips so you are well rested to take on a packed schedule.

The rest of the trip was an eye-opener for me. We travelled for two and a half hours from Durban to cooperatives near Newcastle for our scoping visit. The scheduled meeting with the cooperative groups lasted for merely 30 minutes. In South Africa, the government provided fertile land to the poor for free. All they had to do was fence the property and start their projects. However, there was a noticeable lack of entrepreneurial spirit and the interest to grow as the women demanded assistance from the government for their various needs. The focus seemed to be more on prayer for solace rather than on economic growth or self-sufficiency. The country had gained independence, but there was a palpable sense of unrest and lack of confidence among the people. There were no role models or strong local leadership. Unlike in India, where resources are limited and accessibility is a challenge, in South Africa, the issue was more about building confidence, fostering group dynamics and assisting with business planning. If our women had access to free land, they would use the opportunity and come out of poverty with skill training and financial literacy.

In South Africa, we had to work with the municipality to bring about change, having them as the link to our clients. In India, we do the same but the difference is that our government policies are generally supportive, especially for women, making it easier for organizations like ours to work directly with them, provide training and facilitate market access. The cost for implementation also varied drastically. It was nearly 100 times more in South Africa, so we could not scale the project as rapidly or widely as in India.

Culturally, there were similarities with Indians, such as a belief in superstitions and a tendency to spend heavily on funerals and rituals rather than on constructive purposes. However, a major difference was the prevalence of polygamy—an issue that Indians do not face. There were too many broken families and marginalized women. I knew I had to come up with a solution keeping in mind their cultural nuances.

After my initial scoping, my team and I made several extensive trips to South Africa and interacted with many government officials, including President Mbeki himself. My first meeting with President Mbeki was with Percy and Madhu.

Percy and I made a detailed presentation highlighting the expansion strategy, budget and resources required. After several meetings, it was agreed that a special focus was needed to broaden the base of the Accelerated and Shared Growth Initiative for South Africa, led by Deputy President Mlambo-Ngcuka. This involved addressing the challenges faced by the Second Economy, whose population was around

15–20 million,[4] comprised of the poorest communities, women, youth and physically challenged people. The First Economy, consisting of the whites, the urban and educated, continued to see greater prosperity after the country was freed from apartheid while the poorer, less educated black women and youth, mostly in the rural and peri-urban areas, were struggling to come out of poverty.

Although South Africa had some experience with microfinancing groups and cooperatives, the entry of HIH in 2005 introduced new possibilities for mass mobilization of downtrodden women and entrepreneurship initiatives aimed at improving their lives.

Travelling to South Africa frequently with the HIH India team was a unique experience for me. Food was one of the biggest challenges for us as some of us were vegetarians. We often found ourselves being served dishes like monkey ribs and brains, which were considered delicacies, at dinner buffets. Many nights, I ended up chugging cold chocolate milk and eating warm French fries. Additionally, travelling in South Africa was not considered safe, especially for women. Even though we were put up in good hotels as guests of the government, we were advised not to venture out alone in the evenings and nights.

I also learnt to adapt to South African culture by embracing its nuances, particularly in clothing and mindset, while holding on to my Indian values. By immersing myself in the local environment, I was able to gain deeper insights into their perspectives.

I realized the importance of conducting thorough research

before visiting a new country, including understanding their interests, background, climate, attire and culture. This lesson proved invaluable not only during my travels but also throughout my journey.

❧

In October 2005, the IIC, chaired by President Mbeki, launched a major national programme called Jobs for Growth with the target of creating one million jobs. Percy and I were a part of the interdepartmental working group that hashed out the modalities for the implementation of HIH India's SHG model in South Africa.

In January 2006, the deputy president and all the concerned ministries formed a Central Technical Unit to coordinate the work of 50 local-level teams, each consisting of three members. This covered all the nine provinces of the country with the teams identifying 200 community-based organizations (CBOs)/NGOs to implement the programme at the grassroots level. The goal was to train 1,000 members of these CBOs/NGOs, create 3,00,000 enterprises and generate one million jobs.

My team and I assisted in guiding the programme throughout, from the preparation of the project concept document with a special focus on the identification and training of CBOs to developing the strategy for enterprise development and monitoring the implementation.

3 August 2006 was a red-letter day in the story of HIH India as a memorandum of understanding (MOU) was signed between HIH, led by me, and the Independent Development Trust (IDT), funded by the Government of South Africa. The MOU outlined the deliverables and funding for the project.[5]

This moment was truly exhilarating. I could hardly believe that the work I helped develop in the small city of Kanchipuram had crossed borders all the way to South Africa.

HIH promptly sent trainers to train and educate the members, developed an operation manual for the programme and shared resource materials tailored to the requirements of South Africa. To speed up the progress, Percy agreed to fund two pilot projects. An MOU was signed between HIH and the Mangaung-University of the Orange Free State Community Partnership Programme (MUCPP),[6] primarily to demonstrate the SHG model with grants, training etc. for the groups, train CBOs in project implementation and establish procedures and control systems tailored for South Africa. The model was successfully demonstrated throughout 2007.

In May 2007, IDT and HIH extended the MOU to help in training CBOs and facilitate frequent training and exposure visits to India. In the meantime, HIH South Africa (HIH SA) was formed, and a country director, Sazini Mojapelo, with a team, was appointed to further collaborate with the South African government.

During my visit to South Africa in December 2008, I pointed out the need to sustain the creation of jobs and enterprises by extending microfinance operations through a dedicated microfinance organization. I suggested replicating the BRAC Tanzania model,[7] which had achieved break-even in 24 months. An Enterprise Incubation Fund was created to support and facilitate the growth of income-generating projects into profitable micro and small enterprises.[8]

Percy financed this fund and in December 2012, HIH SA entered into an MOU with the consultancy wing of HIH India, HIH Microfinance Limited—a Section 25 not-for-profit company acquired by me to assist in such international consultancies.[9]

My team had successfully established the HIH SHG model in the challenging environment of South Africa. We were able to bring about a significant change in the attitude of the people towards savings and enterprise creation, which helped create jobs and wealth at a fraction of the cost a government would have incurred to achieve the same results. We formed mixed groups, identified a good local NGO to partner with MUCCP and received government support to work directly with the communities. We provided training on savings, internal rotation of savings, skill development and marketing their produce. Some of the most popular enterprises that we fostered were hairdressing, bead making and footwear businesses.

One of the key takeaways from my first global replication project in South Africa was the varying nature of poverty in different parts of the world. In India, the poor usually do not have access to even the basic necessities. In South Africa, however, people were poor despite having access to facilities and security; they were impoverished as they were unaware of their rights and entitlements. They were not really 'free' and felt rather oppressed. Our model helped them gain a voice at home and in their community.

AFGHANISTAN

There are very few places in the world where the condition of women is worse than Afghanistan. The country ranks 146 out of 157 in the Global Gender Equality Index,[10] with less than 20 per cent of women having work experience outside the home and only 6 per cent receiving education beyond the secondary level.[11]

In the early 2000s, the majority of women in Afghanistan faced abject poverty, domestic violence, illiteracy and ignorance, which were compounded by the constant war and strife that resulted in either the death of the men or forced them to leave the country. This situation left many women fending for themselves with their children. Incidents of stoning to death, punishment for adultery, selling daughters and wives for drugs like opium and other such atrocities were common.

India was among the top five countries assisting in the reconstruction of Afghanistan,[12] committing a few billion dollars not only for infrastructure but also for humanitarian assistance, education and health. The Indian government supported many social projects aimed at improving the lives of the poor and vulnerable, including skill training and other development projects through many NGOs.

In early 2006, HIH received an invitation from President Hamid Karzai for the Afghan Donor Conference in London, which was attended by Percy. Soon after, an Indian delegation was sent to Afghanistan to scope the potential for replicating HIH India's job creation model. The team's report proposed a five-year project to create two million jobs in rural areas and half a million jobs in urban areas of Afghanistan.[13] This led to the establishment of HIH Afghanistan in 2006.

In the first 18 months, HIH India conducted workshops and seminars, working closely with the ministries of the Afghan government. Our workshops centred on the formation of SHGs, the role of skill training and the benefits of entrepreneurship as tools to alleviate poverty. We lobbied with funding agencies for the main project. Some NGOs working in Afghanistan, like Habitat for Humanity, and representatives of community organizations, especially women, were taken to Kanchipuram on exposure visits.

Some of the experiences of our staff from Afghanistan were chilling. During one of their exposure visits to India, I was informed that our accountant had been screaming at night. When we enquired the next morning, he narrated his tragic story. There were 69 people in his village. One morning, the Taliban ordered all of them to stand in a row facing the wall and shot 68 of them. The accountant was miraculously spared as there were no bullets left in the guns. The Taliban told him to flee as Allah had willed him to live! He ran for his life and joined HIH.

∾

A pilot project supported by the Ministry of External Affairs, Government of India, was implemented in 2007–08 to adapt and transfer HIH India's job creation model and skill development initiatives to Afghanistan. The project focussed on community microfinance and enterprise development in the Balkh and Badakhshan provinces in north Afghanistan. These areas had some of the most inaccessible and tough terrains in the country with practically no roads, piped water and electricity.

Following the model of SHGs, savings credit groups (SCGs) were formed to mobilize the masses for enterprise development. In a span of two years, HIH Afghanistan formed 459 SCGs with more than 22,000 members; 47 per cent of these groups had only women members.[14] Mobilizing socially and economically disadvantaged women necessitated the formation of men's groups first to demonstrate the model's effectiveness and gain support from religious leaders.

Owing to the dedication and hard work of the HIH India team led by Usha Somasundaram, my colleague deputed from India, the religious leaders became champions of HIH's work. They helped the organization win the trust and confidence of the community.

Usha had to wait two months before she could arrange a meeting with the 64 religious leaders, known as *mullahs*, who met every Wednesday in the Blue Mosque at Mazar-i-Sharif. While waiting for the meeting, she underwent a crash course in Quranic teachings to explain how HIH's work would not be against any of the tenets of Islam. Her perseverance finally paid off as the mullahs accepted that the women empowerment programme would not create any problems, paving the way for the formation of SCGs.

The initial hurdles seemed insurmountable—some women refused to form groups while others, who were used to receiving grants, could not understand why they needed to repay the loans. Their lack of education also made the training process more difficult. The community blindly trusted the local mullah and went to him for advice on everything. These challenges were overcome with the help of the mullah, who endorsed the HIH model and supported the formation of SCGs. Subsequently, a profit-sharing concept was introduced to facilitate interest-free loans.

We also encouraged the formation of groups of both genders. Including men in these groups helped build a sense of trust with the locals and over time enabled us to work with women in a targeted way. People from the Tadjiks, Hazaras, Uzbeks, Pashtuns and other mixed communities formed groups and engaged in activities like carpet weaving, handicrafts, food items, poultry, tailoring and horticulture.

More than 50 Afghani men and women from the groups and cooperatives visited Kanchipuram over the year, witnessing group activities and success stories in enterprise creation. Apart from skill training, they were trained in social cohesion, group dynamics, finance, savings, accounting and marketing. Soft loans were given to the groups to expand the business with prompt repayment in most cases.

An independent evaluation commissioned by the Indian government in 2010 found that the strategy adopted by HIH was context-relevant, culture-friendly and enhanced the capacity-building measures of the local population. The beneficiaries selected were found to be gender-balanced and inclusive, targeting the population who generally belonged to the bottom of the social pyramid.[15] The SCG group members displayed a high level of participation, transparency and ownership. Most importantly, the evaluation commended HIH for the effective linkages with the local governments that ensured the sustainability of the project.

One Afghani staff member faced the usual problem of his house being marked for takeover by the local insurgents. Because of the goodwill established with the community, HIH escalated this to the local provincial governor, Atah, who informed the insurgents that HIH people were not to be touched. Managing a project of this nature, in a constant state of fear, was an experience of a lifetime for the HIH staff.

⁂

The success of HIH Afghanistan Organization's (HIH AO) initial projects led to the development of the Afghanistan Rural Enterprise Development Programme (AREDP), funded by the World Bank and coordinated by the Ministry of Rural Rehabilitation and Development (MRRD) of Afghanistan. HIH AO entered into an MOU with the MRRD to prepare a National Enterprise Development Programme, focussing on the mass mobilization of communities into entrepreneurship—an adapted version of the SHG model of HIH in Tamil Nadu. With a budget of $580 million, the programme aimed to create at least two million jobs over 10 years through community-based enterprises.[16]

The deputy minister of MRRD sent a letter to the deputy chief of mission in the Indian Embassy, appreciating the initiative of the Government of India in funding the pilot segment of the project initiated by HIH in northern Afghanistan, the results of which provided the basis for the initiatives incorporated in the final AREDP.

The lesson we learnt was that any project undertaken would require the organization involved to patiently work with the local communities and understand its cultural nuances to sustain the programmes.

Few places make you appreciate your homeland even more. Afghanistan was one such country for me. Implementing a project amidst gunfire, unexpected bombings and extreme weather conditions was a very risky proposition. Some of my staff could not adapt to these changes after coming from the relative security of India. Despite these challenges, our work in Afghanistan remains a testament to our solid model.

It is worth mentioning that in 2021, after the Taliban's takeover of Afghanistan, an article in a popular Indian newspaper by Shri Jayant Prasad, former Indian ambassador to Afghanistan, mentioned HIH's successful model, stating that these should continue in a post-Taliban world to foster a sense of belonging and entrepreneurship among women.[17]

BRAZIL

The Inter-American Development Bank (IDB) was established in the 1990s to finance development projects in both the public and private sectors in Latin America and the Caribbean. Between 2005 and 2019, the bank funded $189 billion worth of projects.[18]

Percy knew Donald F. Terry, the president of the bank and invited him to send a team to India in early 2008.

Svante Persson, a senior executive of the bank, along with Pejman Altafi, a consultant to HIH, visited Kanchipuram and were quite impressed with our job creation model. Percy and I commissioned a scoping study for Brazil—the idea was to look at how the poor were earning their livelihoods and how the Indian model could be adapted to encourage saving habits among them. We also wanted to focus on skill development, training and marketing to improve their incomes and access further funds from microfinance institutions.

My visit to Brazil was starkly different from the visits to South Africa. The flight to Sao Paolo was one of the longest as I had to fly from Chennai to Washington, D.C. via Europe and then to Brazil. Language was one of the first barriers there. English was sparsely spoken and airport signage was only in Portuguese.

I vividly remember losing my balance on the escalator at the airport. A kind-hearted man saved me with his quick reflexes or else I would have ended up with a few broken bones at least!

His act of generosity left me amazed and overwhelmed with gratitude. I realized that even though we belonged to two diverse worlds and spoke different languages, we were connected to each other by virtues like empathy, which bind all of us together into a single fraternity called humanity.

⁂

Our field visits to the *favelas* (slums or ghettos) in Sao Paolo and along the promenades of Rio were overwhelming. It reminded me of my early days in Kanchipuram when children were rampantly employed in silk weaving looms. Drawing parallels between India and Brazil was easier than with South Africa. The economic conditions were similar, but the rich-poor divide was more pronounced. In Brazil, children would drop out of school after an average of two and a half years due to parental abuse and easy accessibility to drugs and alcohol.[19] Despite this grim situation, the biggest upside of their culture was the communal love for sports, especially football.

Upon studying what the microfinance institutions (MFIs) were offering there, I realized that no one was focussing on the convergence of government programmes and savings. We included this aspect in our initiatives, which was appreciated by the community. It was necessary to adapt the training to suit their cultural nuances; we scheduled the sessions keeping in mind the timings of the football games and included cultural components for discussion so they could relate to us better.

The women in Brazil were very enamoured by us Indians and our *bindis* as a Brazilian primetime show on Indians, called *Caminho das Indias*, was very popular back then. This helped them relate to us and accept the trainings we offered.

⁂

Structured as a trust, HIH India had limitations as we could not lend to women entrepreneurs at scale. By 2006, we had close to 3,00,000 women in need of microloans but could not cater to this need.

So, by late 2006, I had registered a new company, Hand in Hand Microfinance Limited (HIHMFL), to undertake microfinance operations and enable the women of the SHGs to access further credit for expanding their business activities. The company could also assume knowledge-transfer activities, especially to take the HIH job creation model worldwide. It was through this institution that we replicated the HIH model as a pilot in Brazil.

The team realized that while Brazil had abundant resources, the level of poverty, especially in the urban slum areas, was very high. There was no concept of savings and investment in enterprises, and some microfinance firms charged interest rates as high as 47 per cent.[20] To address this, we decided to concentrate on the north-eastern coastal areas of Brazil, supported by funding from the Multilateral Investment Fund (MIF) of IDB and technical assistance from HIH.

HIH developed the training modules in Brazilian Portuguese and sent teams to train the trainers. HIH assumed the responsibility of evaluating the progress and suggesting corrective measures. Visao Mundial, a local NGO, organized GoLD (Group of Local Opportunity and Development) cohorts through local volunteers called Agents for Development for the sensitization and further training of group members. We decided that the groups would have both men and women, given the large number of youth requiring support.

∞

Percy funded the initial scoping and study on how we could replicate our model in Brazil. It was then on me to convince the top brass of IDB for further funding.

I deliberated on how I would sell my ideas to the representatives of the 25 member countries of IDB. In the last week of June 2008, I presented a proposal to the representatives of the member countries in Washington, highlighting a multistakeholder partnership model for poverty alleviation. I also fielded a rapid round of questions from top bureaucrats of those countries.

The members were impressed by the cost-effective model of providing sustainable employment and the full participation of the relevant local organizations. The project was approved with funding from the MIF of IDB, the first in its history of SSC. The Reduction of Poverty through Regional Integration of Local Business Capacities (REDES) project was thus born, covering coastal districts of north-eastern Brazil. It was a deeply emotional moment for me as it marked our expansion to a third country besides India and had been institutionalized with funding from one of the world's largest development sector banks.

HIH's global replication was entirely process-driven, from exploration missions, sensitization workshops and intensive training sessions for staff members and trainers. It also included exposure visits of Visao Mundial's top management and the operational team members to India and the production of all operational and other manuals in the local language, which Visao Mundial modified to suit the local context and bring in innovations.

HIH relentlessly emphasized the importance of forming partnerships at every level—from individual groups to the state governments. HIH conducted a mid-term evaluation in early 2011 to make further improvements. The evaluation revealed that income levels had indeed gone up, with the GoLD members getting loan assistance from group savings and MFIs at very low interest rates for the first time in their lives and reinvesting their savings to make their enterprises more successful. Raynald Miranda, National Facilitator of the GoLD methodology at Visao Mundial, appreciated our efforts, stating, 'People feel more empowered as they have accumulated savings of $2,50,000 over these last two and a half years. I acknowledge with thanks the initial capacity building and handholding support provided by Hand in Hand to our initiative.'

The biggest achievement was the power of togetherness seen amongst the members. In January 2015, Svante Persson of IDB acknowledged that HIH's poverty reduction model successfully proved that social innovations from Asia could be adapted to Brazil, highlighting how the project had generated income opportunities for 50,000 people in 10 states of north-east Brazil using a combination of technical assistance, access to finance and linkages to markets and industries in relevant sectors.[21]

At the Livelihoods Asia Summit in New Delhi, 2014, Persson shared the insights from HIH's pilot project in Brazil. He acknowledged the effectiveness of SSC but stressed the importance of customizing methods to suit local culture and overcome obstacles. He mentioned patience and flexibility as the keys to success.

Persson also underscored the need to form strategic partnerships with local grassroots organizations as they help expand, strengthen, integrate and institutionalize the job creation project. Furthermore, he highlighted the necessity for local ownership of the project by these groups and noted the importance of fostering cross-sector cooperation between the public and private sectors that should be assiduously nurtured. Finally, Persson stressed the importance of simplicity and cost-effectiveness in project design, advocating for close monitoring and timely course corrections to ensure success.

∽

The success of the pilot in Brazil led to a second project titled 'Poverty Reduction through Regional Integration of Local Capacities' in the poorest areas of Honduras, El Salvador, Guatemala, Nicaragua and Costa Rica being approved by the IDB in September 2010.[22] HIHMFL executed a Letter of Understanding with World Vision (Visao Mundial), the project executing agency, in July 2011, agreeing to render technical assistance for the next 18 months.[23]

In 2010, Hemantha Pamarthy, the managing director of HIHMFL, and I had an opportunity to meet the president of IDB, Luis Alberto Moreno, who was visiting India to attend the World Economic Forum meeting. He acknowledged the work done by HIH in lifting people out of extreme poverty across the world, stating that HIH was being invited to several Central and Latin American countries to share its developmental experience and empower individuals overcome poverty. This partnership would go a long way to strengthen the developmental sector in these countries and also promote South-South dialogue. This remains a solid testimony to our work!

CAMBODIA

The experience of working in South Africa, Afghanistan and Brazil encouraged me and my colleagues to consider taking the HIH job creation model to other South-east Asian countries. Upon analysing the various parameters of poverty, per capita gross domestic product (GDP), growth, access to credit, education, livelihood options and many more, Cambodia appeared to require a programme similar to those implemented in the other countries.

Further discussions revealed some NGOs already working in Cambodia, leading HIH India to seek the support of Percy and HIH Sweden to launch a project in collaboration with a local NGO partner, the Cambodian Rural Development Team (CRDT). The partnership was coordinated by the Asian Institute of Technology, Bangkok, which had considerable experience working with several NGOs in the region.

In the meantime, HIHMFL was converted into an international consultancy, Hand in Hand Consulting Services Private Limited (HIHCSPL), to take the HIH model to other countries. Thus in July 2012, we began our initiatives in Cambodia, in the provinces of Kratie and Stung Treng. The aim of the two-year project was to create 5,000 jobs by forming 155 SHGs.

❧

Our trip to Cambodia was enriched by the experiences the local people shared with us. While the terrain was very different from the countries we visited in the southern hemisphere, it also felt more familiar as it was closer to home. The locals were extremely hard working but needed a catalyst to bring them out of poverty. They were very open to learning and ready to adapt to the changing times.

Following the horrendous Pol Pot regime genocide, the population in Cambodia was predominantly young and grateful to be alive. Their livelihoods revolved around the Mekong River that flowed through the region. They were waiting for opportunities that would unleash their potential and provide financial independence. However, the focus on education, especially for girls, was very limited.

The sight of intravenous medical tubes connected to mango trees[24] was shocking and provided an insight into the sparse access to health services, revealing a stark lack of medical infrastructure. People had to travel to Bangkok for treatment for critical illnesses. There was great potential for our model to work with support from local partners.

While the CRDT had relevant experience in forming community-based organizations locally, these were only for receiving grants and other assistance; the SHG model was new to Cambodia. The penetration of financial institutions like banks was very low and the existing microfinance institutions had very rigid financing and collection norms while also charging uneconomical interest rates.[25]

With very few jobs in the formal sector, more than 60 per cent of the population were self-employed. They had low and irregular incomes and consequently, low savings and investment, leading to a never-ending cycle of poverty and deprivation.[26] The main sources of employment in the two provinces were agriculture and fishing, and both were seasonal. There was an urgent need to find other sources of employment.

Drawing from our experiences in other countries, we organized capacity-building exercises systematically; CRDT, though new to the concepts of SHGs and savings model, quickly grasped the ideas, facilitating better group organizations.

The model was modified to suit the Cambodian context,

including adjustments in the targeted population, group training timings and duration, bank linkage and composition of members. For example, the top and bottom quintiles in the villages were left out as the top would dominate the group and the bottom would not be able to contribute time or money for the group meetings and savings. The groups also had male members, as there was greater gender equality in the Cambodian society in terms of participation and role of men. However, the lack of accessible banks made it difficult to open bank accounts and store cash, which was a given in the other countries.

Despite the hurdles, the HIH team could see the enthusiasm of the people and by October 2014, the project had generated 5,690 jobs through 191 SHGs, with 1,138 enterprises initiated by the groups. Increased incomes through the initiatives resulted in savings increasing substantially.[27] To expand the activities Hand in Hand Cambodia and a microfinance entity, Mekong Rural Credit Operator, were established. Value chains[28] in rice and vegetable cultivation and poultry and piggery were started to consolidate the gains and provide training to the families.

An independent evaluation commissioned by HIH in June 2013[29] confirmed that a majority of the targeted groups were engaged in some form of economic activity, with group savings averaging $290. A full 30 per cent used internal savings to finance their enterprises, which was an absolutely new development and encouraged more savings and investment.

I visited Cambodia four times and could see that while incomes were low and facilities minimal, the women and the groups were very enthusiastic and thankful for the training and support, asking for further assistance. The contribution from CRDT staff members enabled the microcredit entity with a corpus of $1,00,000 to finance income-generating activities.[30]

In 2019, HIH Sweden extended funding for a new project named Cambodia SHG Project for Increased Livelihoods with a budget of $1,26,000. The project yielded immediate results; income increases ranged from $250 to $750 in groups, and individual members' savings, in some cases, reached up to $100, with an average of $25 to $50. Hundreds of enterprises were started with an attempt to diversify the activities.[31]

HIH Cambodia's journey was very different from the other global replication models as we had limited funding for the project. Cambodia has not been a country of interest to global foundations or MIFs. While the Mekong's prominent presence in the landscape had generated some interest in climate change-related projects, addressing poverty was not a priority for global funds.

In this scenario, we managed to achieve significant impact with just a fraction of the resources allocated to projects in other countries like South Africa. I am very proud that a project focussing on entrepreneurship is currently ongoing with support from Geneva, Switzerland through Hand in Hand Switzerland, a fundraising entity I set up in 2013. The goal of HIH Cambodia was to reduce poverty by investing in the capacity development of women from poor households, helping them secure and strengthen their livelihoods. Over the past 10 years, the Cambodian team has created 14,000 jobs and formed 321 SHGs. Currently there are several on-going projects focussing on job creation for women and entrepreneurship through spectacle sales.

SRI LANKA

A crucial element of HIH's interventions in the other countries was the scoping studies that preceded implementation. The main objective of these studies was to understand the socioeconomic conditions in the host country to zero in on the poorest areas where the job creation model would have the maximum impact.

Sri Lanka was one of the countries where I strongly believed our job creation model could be replicated. In Sri Lanka, Hand in Hand Consulting Services Private Limited (HIHCSPL) selected Nuwara Eliya, one of the poorest areas consisting of mainly tea plantation workers, for the scoping study. The average daily wage was a meagre Lankan Rupee (LKR) 195, while the poorest quality rice cost LKR 90 per kilogram. Malnutrition, illiteracy, high suicide rates, poor sanitary and living conditions were forcing the people to become poorer, with the rate of poverty increasing from 22 per cent in 2002 to 34 per cent in 2007.[32] To take the initiative further, I started a not-for-profit company called HIH Lanka in 2011 to support communities in post-war Sri Lanka with community and poverty alleviation projects. I knew once again that I had to take a partnership approach as I wanted to understand the sentiments of the communities. We chose Sevalanka and Berendina as our partners and operated a small pilot in the districts of Vavuniya and Mannar.

At this time, the United Methodist Committee on Relief approached HIHCSPL to strengthen the capacity of its staff in the formation and management of SHGs and improve the livelihoods of the poor. An eight-member team underwent intensive 10-day training at Kanchipuram, resulting in the organization of Village Livelihoods Groups in Sri Lanka. The training exercise continued with many participants learning about the job creation model for the first time.

A group of war widows participated in a five-day training programme and expressed interest in weaving, organic farming and solid waste management. The delegations were enthusiastic and HIH wanted to concentrate on the Tamil-majority areas, which for various reasons the government could not agree.

I am very passionate about replicating our successful model in Sri Lanka as women there, very similar to those in South India but with harsher backgrounds, have immense potential to thrive with entrepreneurship as their backbone. Unfortunately the government preferred for-profit structures instead of not-for-profit and we didn't have the flexibility to implement projects that we felt would address the needs of the women there. We are still looking out for partners who can help us replicate our model here.

MYANMAR

Considering that a majority of the families in Myanmar are self-employed,[33] HIHCSPL started a project in 2013 in the Sut San area of Bogalay Township in the Irrawaddy region of Myanmar. This collaboration with Swanyee Development Foundation, a local NGO, was aimed at helping families devastated by Cyclone Nargis rebuild their lives. We chose Myanmar due to its similarities with other countries in South-east Asia where we could provide access to credit and skill training to the poor and help them diversify their livelihoods.

In 2013, I visited Myanmar with Srinivas Krishnaswamy, the then managing director of HIHCSPL. The villages we scoped could be reached only after a two-and-a-half-hour-long bamboo boat ride. Our days used to start by 8 a.m. and ended post 9 p.m. The environment was rather hostile as there were restrictions on mobility; everything we scoped and implemented was under supervision.

By October 2014, HIH had created 58 SHGs and 522 enterprises, creating 2,610 jobs.[34] Each group was given a financial assistance of $150, in addition to training on group dynamics, financial literacy and enterprise management. Upon the conclusion of the initial project funding, securing further grants became limited. Without the backup of a multilateral fund or government support, it was challenging to complete the project at scale as the other countries. The security concerns proved a roadblock for our growth as well. Nonetheless, HIH is continuing its efforts to secure higher funds and lobbying with the government to make the SHGs the cornerstone for all financial inclusion policies.

EAST AFRICA

HIH International had started Hand in Hand East Africa in 2010 to implement the job creation and enterprise development model in consultation with HIH India and HIHCSPL. A scoping study revealed that financial literacy and skills among the members of the collectives already formed was poor. The training given was inadequate and sporadic, necessitating the development of business skills. Supply chain and logistics were not developed, with most enterprises operating at the bottom end of the value chain and facing limited access to capital and risk mitigation products like microinsurance.

The HIH team planned activities to address these gaps and identified sectors where value chains could be created by forming SHGs who in turn would be provided with skill training and financing. Based on my experiences, I gave inputs on the scoping study and encouraged the formation of an enterprise incubation fund for SHGs in East Africa.

I was also invited in April 2013 to speak at the launch of Papua New Guinea's Centre for Excellence in Financial Inclusion, co-financed by the Asian Development Bank, the Australian Agency for International Development and the Government of Papua New Guinea. I explained the evolution of our model over 10 years and its success in financing 9,15,000 enterprises with funding of $183 million. The Prime Minister of Papua New Guinea, Peter O Neill, promised to take up our model for enterprise development.

~

During our journey of global replication, in each country, my team of experts and I follow certain basic steps—a scoping study is done to see the ground realities in the country and to decide on the strategy that would work. This scoping involves reviewing secondary literature and the government policies before travelling. Post-travel, we meet with local government officials, grassroots-level institutions and clients. Adopting this multistakeholder approach enables us to understand the limitations and benefits of the ongoing programmes and develop some ideas on what new initiatives can address the aspirations of the communities. This ensures that our project is never some cosmetic changes but well thought out approaches, whether it be waiting for the mullahs patiently in Afghanistan or bringing in men in the groups in Cambodia.

Local institutions are identified with support from the local government (we were lucky to have this support in all our projects) to carry out the mobilization and monitoring tasks and the community is trained to own the project. Our strategy involves translating the enterprise development training from India to these countries. We have one person from India working with their counterpart in the respective country for the duration of the project. They work together to customize the approaches to address any cultural and language barriers. The field pilot test outcomes are documented and training manuals based on the outcomes are prepared by HIH India, which are later used by partner organizations.

HIH provides technical support, training, exposure visits to India and conducts mid-term evaluations. Alternative channels are used in countries where banking facilities are not widespread; HIH tries to bring in microfinance institutions to sustain credit flow to matured groups. Enterprise creation is central to our efforts as only they can lead to sustained development. With almost a billion families earning less than $2 a day,[35] it is critical that such efforts are nurtured at the global level.

In all models involving women or the poor, the standard practice was to form groups, expose them to finance and facilitate their growth. However, in many cases, enterprise creation fell by the wayside due to various reasons. For instance, no time and effort was spent on the social aspects of group cohesion, resulting in groups existing only for accessing grants from the government or donors. Moreover, no training was provided in enterprise creation, modern management practices or finance management and no efforts were made to link these groups to regular, cheaper funding sources like banks, either due to the absence of such sources or the reluctance of agencies forming the groups to lose their clients.

I addressed these challenges by leveraging the social capital of the groups and aligning it with the economic strength of enterprises. I carefully matched the needs of the people with efficient management principles to maximize the value for the money spent with the organization, willing to let go of the people once they reach some scale to be nurtured by MFIs and banks.

I advocated the formation of MFIs by the creators of the groups to ensure mission alignment with the core objective of poverty eradication. This approach created a vibrant and workable model for poverty alleviation across the world, gaining acceptance from major financing agencies such as the World Bank in Afghanistan, IDB in Brazil and the Asian Development Bank in India.

Here I want to dive into a case study to elaborate a success story in Cambodia.

SUCCESSFUL VEGETABLE BUSINESS—CAMBODIA

> Ms Yan Sopheak, aged 51, resides in Kou Loab village, Kou Loab commune, Chetr Borei district, Kratie province. She completed her education up to the ninth-grade level and is married with four children, including one daughter. Her family's primary occupations involve cultivating vegetables at home and running vegetable market stalls within the provincial market. These endeavours receive support from international organizations as well as the Provincial Department of Agriculture, Forestry and Fisheries.
>
> On 20 May 2023, she became a registered member of the SHG named Kosh Andeitty. Through this

association, she gains access to additional technical guidance from HIH Cambodia, which encompasses agricultural techniques, finance management, vision development and entrepreneurial skills aimed at enhancing her farming and business ventures. An active participant in the SHG, she has managed to save $800 during the current year and obtained a loan of $1,000 when initiating her business, as reported by group representatives.

Through her combined farming and market stall operations, she achieves an annual income of up to $11,462 while incurring a total cost of $5,500, resulting in a profit of $5,962. She allocates some of these earnings to expand her business by purchasing land and supporting her children's education.

Since joining the SHG and accessing loans to enhance her existing business, her family's economic prospects have considerably flourished. She acknowledges that the HIH Cambodia project supported by HIH India/Sweden has significantly contributed to her family's economic advancement by providing innovative business ideas and essential skills training.

'Do not go where the path may lead; go instead where there is no path and leave a trail.'

—Ralph Waldo Emerson

Emerson's philosophy is precisely what I focussed on when globally replicating HIH India's model. It is not often that an NGO born in India is recognized globally for its work and invited by other countries to implement projects. Having this opportunity and successfully implementing projects globally validated our model as truly successful.

6

CREATIVE INSTITUTION BUILDING

'You may have to fight a battle more than once to win it.'

—Margaret Thatcher

Resilience is the ability to rise every time there is a fall—easier said than done. Individuals have an infinite capacity to excel on a personal level, but creating institutions with the same ethos of 'never say die' requires enormous talent and perseverance.

HIH, as an institution, has grown from its humble beginnings in the tiny Emma House to its present form, covering several continents and overcoming many challenges along the way. The story is one of constant institution creation and building things from scratch.

Over the last two decades, I have created 10 different entities, each designed to cater to the different needs of the community and to ensure the sustainability of HIH India.

HAND IN HAND CONSULTING SERVICES PRIVATE LIMITED

When I joined HIH in 2004, it was a single entity running few crèches, a parcel scheme for the tribal and poor families, a tailoring unit mainly for training poor women and a small school with few children.

I quickly established the operations for extending credit to the newly formed SHGs and realized that the operations could not be sustained without a larger organizational structure and access to institutional finance. Donor money can only take you so far and overdependence on it could lead to complications later, as seen in many foreign-funded entities.

My core expertise was in microfinance and I felt that it was necessary to start an MFI to meet the credit needs of the SHGs who suffered once their financial needs increased. Their operations would dry up if funds were not made available quickly as the banking system was not tuned towards helping these first-generation small entrepreneurs.

To address this gap, I started Hand in Hand Microfinance Limited, which was registered under the Companies Act 1956, and the first board meeting of the company was held on 22 December 2006. To operate as a Non-Banking Finance Company (NBFC), the Reserve Bank of India (RBI) prescribed an initial capital of ₹20 million, which had to come from local promoters and groups. The RBI was wary of any funds routed through NGOs already receiving foreign funding; if foreign money had to be used for starting the operations, the initial capital required was ₹1 billion. This was a significant hurdle, which I overcame through an innovative method of raising capital directly from the women of the SHGs.

The women were formed into mutual benefit trusts

(MBTs), with each individual contributing as low as ₹3,000 to higher amounts based on their capability. Six such trusts were formed, collectively bringing in funds of ₹21 million—sufficient to apply for the license from the regulator.[1] This model could have been a path-breaking step in financing poor families worldwide but unfortunately, the unique nature of this fundraising approach did not get the regulator's approval easily. In the middle of 2008, I explored another method to bring in the capital by involving the employees of HIH through a for-profit tax-paying trust. However, mobilizing the full amount required proved to be a challenge.

In December 2008, my board and I wisely decided to put the decision on NBFC operations on hold. We shifted our focus to consultancy and collaboration assignments in India and abroad to spread the HIH model. In January 2010, HIHMFL was transformed into a private limited company in line with its new objectives and renamed Hand in Hand Microfinance Private Limited. A new chief operating officer (COO) was appointed and the company quickly secured consultancy assignments with organizations like AIDS Prevention and Control Project-Voluntary Health Services on health initiatives, International Crops Research Institute for the Semi-Arid Tropics, Hyderabad, for rain-fed agricultural projects and the United Methodist Committee on Relief in Sri Lanka for training microfinance specialists. The company also supported the establishment of Hand in Hand Sri Lanka in early 2011. It was effectively utilized for all knowledge-based capacity-building exercises on behalf of HIH. In mid-2012, the company entered into an agreement with HIH International to support job creation activities in South and South-east Asia.

A tripartite agreement was signed with the CRDT and the Asian Institute of Technology, Thailand, to take up job creation activities in Cambodia. A similar agreement was executed with HIH India for a project in Myanmar. The following year, the company executed three consultancy projects for the German organization Deutsche Gesellschaft für Internationale Zusammenarbeit (GIZ). In June 2013, HIHMFL signed a cooperation agreement with the Swanyee Development Foundation, an NGO from Myanmar, to undertake job creation activities in Myanmar with financial assistance from HIH International.

In March 2014, Hand in Hand Microfinance Private Limited changed its name to Hand in Hand Consulting Services Private Limited to reflect the changed scope of its operations. With the support of HIH International, HIHCSPL helped HIH India in organizing the first Global Social Entrepreneurship Programme, helmed by Prof. Kash Rangan of Harvard Business School (HBS) and Sohel Karim of Socient Associates, a social enterprise consulting firm. The first cohort witnessed 65 participants from around the globe engaging in a week-long immersive experience at the Great Lakes Institute of Management near Chennai. Since then, three such programmes have been held to foster social entrepreneurship.

HIHCSPL continues to support the Cambodian project and also takes up assignments for Belstar Microfinance Private Limited to study Micro, Small & Medium Enterprises loans and mobile-based customer-oriented loans. While I could not initiate NBFC operations, establishing HIHCSPL enabled us to create an exclusive organization for consultancy assignments and also provided the flexibility needed for the operating teams at HIH to concentrate on their core developmental activities. Additionally, HIHCSPL helped the NGO to take up evaluation studies independently.

HAND IN HAND INCLUSIVE DEVELOPMENT AND SERVICES

The Companies Act 2013 provides for a not-for-profit company that can combine the advantages of a corporate structure with a charitable, socially relevant purpose; these companies are designed to plough back the profits generated into the company rather than distributing them to shareholders or investors. As per Section 25 of the Companies Act 1956, similar to Section 8 under the Companies Act 2013, this structure provides an organized alternative to forming charitable trusts, which have their own bye-laws and accounting standards.[2] The advantage of a Section 8 company is that grants from donors can be used for capital purposes and as collateral for accessing bank loans. These companies can also accept user fees from communities for project initiatives. Thus, with a small capital base contributed by myself and other shareholders, the company could access larger funds and develop a robust model for its undertakings.

The new company, The Helping Hand Micro Finance & Services, quickly identified opportunities in areas such as solid waste management, drinking water supply, small housing repairs and the management of reverse osmosis water treatment plants. The timing was also perfect; urban local bodies were struggling to manage their daily waste and were seeking organizations capable of employing the personnel needed to collect segregated waste door-to-door and operate waste treatment plants that produced biogas from the compostable waste and recycled other waste materials like plastic, paper and glass.

Starting with small localities, the company undertook several projects for colleges, universities and other institutions, including factories. It developed innovative solutions such as using compostable waste to produce biogas that could be used to power a generator, providing electricity for the street lights in the local bodies without any expense in Mahabalipuram, near Chennai. The company also built resource recovery parks to recycle reusable waste, which became good training centres for local bodies and students. For this initiative, HIH emerged as the runner-up in the BBC World Challenge Contest held in Amsterdam in 2011.[3] In 2012, its entry in the World Environment Day challenge hosted by the UNEP won the 'Most Creative, Unique and Fun' prize.[4] In 2019, the programme won the award for waste management at the National Swachhata Meet at Delhi.

NABARD was already assisting many watershed projects through HIH and the new company started implementing some of these projects. Besides maintaining the reverse osmosis plants built with donor funds, the company launched pure drinking water supply schemes, selling water cans at highly subsidized rates. In mid-2013, the company changed its name to Hand in Hand Inclusive Development and Services to reflect its new role as a not-for-profit company, but without the financing operations.

My objective behind establishing this company was clear. The NGO, HIH, would focus on ultra-poor women—empower them through financial and functional literacy programmes, entrepreneurship, vocational training and access to savings products to make them 'economically active' to avail further financing by charging minimal interest and linking up with government subsidies whenever possible—while the Section 8 company would function as an intermediary for microfinance, charging interest up to 24–26 per cent. As the profits would not be taxed, they could be reinvested into the NGO for its various initiatives. Being a not-for-profit company, it could also leverage donor funds to raise more finance and take up a wide range of developmental activities.

This structure not only helped in the scaling of the charitable activities but also created an institution that could undertake economically sustainable activities at reasonable prices with no predatory pricing or aggressive marketing—hallmarks of a purely for-profit enterprise.

BELSTAR MICROFINANCE LIMITED

After completing my three-week training programme on microfinance conducted by the Boulder Institute of Microfinance in Turin, Italy, I noted my key takeaways from the programme for Percy, which were:

- Microfinance is a commercial proposition. Worldwide, there are numerous successful MFIs such as the Equity Bank, Kenya; BRAC, Bangladesh; BancoSol, Bolivia; and Bank Rakyat Indonesia.
- The microfinance industry is gaining much attention after Compartamos Banco in Mexico made a huge profit with a return on equity of 40 per cent. Its stock was oversubscribed by 13 times!
- MFIs across the globe have become profitable with just 5,000 clients.
- The rate of interest varies from 26–100 per cent, with the average being 31 per cent.
- Training, perceived as critical by almost all the NGOs, may not be essential.

I concluded that it was necessary for HIH to transform itself into a legal entity to continuously attract equity from the market, gain legitimacy and offer financial services beyond mere lending.

As a charitable organization, it was becoming difficult for HIH to raise funds in bulk for on-lending, and raising risk capital was also not possible. The ability to make profits while maintaining the ethos of working for the poor would be only possible if a new commercially-oriented institution was created.

Thus, in late 2008, I acquired Belstar Investment and Finance Private Limited, a Bangalore-based MFI already registered with the RBI, with mine, my relatives' and staff's funds.

What I could not achieve by starting a new grassroots-level organization, I could accomplish by acquiring an existing institution. I was looking for equity partners and had lined up organizations like SIDBI and Opportunity International. However, we couldn't agree on the right valuation. Percy supported us by bringing in organizations like the International Finance Corporation, Norfund from Norway, Swedfund from Sweden and Aavishkaar, a venture capital firm from Mumbai. The MBTs I had formed earlier were federated into the Sarvam Mutual Benefit Trust. This apex body represented around 120 MBTs of HIH, about 33,000 SHGs and more than 4,50,000 women indirectly.

❧

The MBT model was pioneered by institutions like SKS Microfinance, Spandana and Bandhan, which started as not-for-profit microfinance institutions to reach the last mile in financing the rural and urban poor who could not access the normal banking channels easily but needed funds for their small enterprise activities and personal needs. MFIs met an important demand segment whose only other option was the local money lender. The growth of the SHGs or joint liability group model enabled risk spreading and ensured prompt repayment of loans. Not-for-profit MFIs could start making profits and saw a huge opportunity in scaling up with outside private equity and other finances, provided they could float for-profit entities regulated by the central bank. The catch was in their inability to plough the profits directly into the equity of the new for-profit entity as that would affect their not-for-profit tax-free status. Thus, the concept of MBTs of the beneficiaries of the microloans was born.

The difference between Belstar and the other pioneers of the MBT model was that the funds of Belstar's MBTs were not the accumulated surplus of the MFI but the savings and surplus of individual members of the community. They would be part owners in the new company and entitled to the benefits of any capital appreciation. Whereas other MFIs had equity routed through a few MBTs formed for the purpose, Belstar started with about 120 MBTs, each representing about 200–300 SHGs. However, not all could be direct shareholders in the NBFC, which is a private limited company, so the Sarvam Mutual Benefit Trust would be the investor in Belstar.

This was a completely new model for an NBFC-MFI; NBFCs were all formed with private equity and their operations were completely commercial and profit-oriented. NBFC-MFIs followed the same model; private funds were brought in as equity and the operations were purely commercial. However, the borrowers were from the poorest sections of the community who could not be exploited for commercial profits endlessly.

The dilemma was to align the needs of the poor with that of the financial system. My model provided a via media; the process of forming the SHGs, providing them training on financial inclusion and skill for enterprise development and offering continuous support would be the basis for the loans. The focus was not on mere lending and capturing the cream of the market but the development of the family, group and the community as a whole, with the NBFC-MFI meeting the crucial need for timely finance. Profits were incidental but necessary to sustain the operations.

2010 was a watershed period for microfinance companies in India. Due to the overdrive of a few ambitious companies and their aggressive marketing and collection methods, borrowers in Andhra Pradesh, unable to bear it, started ending their lives, leading to a major public outcry for stringent control and monitoring of NBFCs. As a result, some companies had to suspend all their activities when the Andhra Pradesh government enacted a law requiring statutory approvals from local authorities for all operations including setting an interest rate ceiling. The challenge was in the perception of other investors, especially the international financing entities, who were uncomfortable with the community ownership model after the Andhra Pradesh crisis. They felt that there were reputational risks due to the practices of the other MFIs, where promoters gained from the capital appreciation and leverage, not the community.

During this time, I enlisted the Credit Rating Information Services of India Limited (CRISIL) to conduct a governance study. They identified 16 areas for improvement in our current model. Primarily, they suggested we return the borrowed money to the women at a fair valuation. After obtaining the valuation from Religare, we returned the money at fair value to all those who had invested in Sarvam. This proved to be a laborious exercise since the women were present in different localities and each return required detailed paper work. But we traced back to each MBT and woman to ensure the money was returned, provided each of them a receipt and closing every account. After completing this procedure, went back to CRISIL for another governance study and modified the Sarvam's deed to reflect the necessary changes.

Despite these efforts, 2009 and 2010 were challenging for me and my team. The money collected from the SHGs was lying with the MBTs and Sarvam but could not be brought in as further equity because the other shareholders were not providing consent.

Following the Andhra Pradesh crisis, the RBI intervened and formed the Malegam Committee to suggest corrective measures. Formed in October 2010, the committee made a slew of important recommendations covering the interest rate, capital adequacy of MFIs, their sources of funding, loan amounts and income levels of the borrowers, the percentage of loans to be given for income-generating activities, the proportion of such lending in the company's total portfolio and the linking of all such loans through a credit bureau to monitor the loans sourced by the clients. This was a welcome development that enabled Belstar to reorganize its activities.

We were on the lookout for further equity funding from the market but it was not until 2013 that I could channel the money collected from the SHGs through the MBTs into the core business of microlending, with bank and other lenders also pitching in.

From the beginning, Belstar had clear policies on customer engagement and practices. Unlike other MFIs, Belstar insisted on customers paying their dues at the branches, rather than sending collection teams to the borrowers' residences; this ensured that the dignity of the customers was never compromised. The general practice of other MFIs was to source business through agents or staff, centralize all processing through use of IT, manage collections through collection agents and to the maximum extent possible, securitize the assets and keep expanding irrespective of any real need for financing or use for income generation.

Belstar's approach was fundamentally different. While the other MFIs concentrated their lending through Joint Liability Groups, Belstar insisted on forming SHGs, training them on group cohesion, group dynamics, financial literacy, numeracy and accounting skills and encouraging the use of their own savings for productive activities. Loans from Belstar were intended to help these groups scale up. The branch concept was introduced so that customers could come together to sign all the documents at the time of disbursement, ensuring that all members were genuine. The branch became the nodal point for repayment also thus removing one of the major complaints against MFIs.

When Belstar was looking for investors to further scale up the operations, a Belgian investor expressed interest to invest. The breakthrough finally came in 2016 when Muthoot Finance Limited, a Kerala-based gold loan lending company, invested in Belstar and bought out the shares of the other investors. This was followed by investments from Maj Invest, Denmark, in 2018 and Affirma Capital, USA, in 2021. There was no looking back for Belstar after these strategic investments!

Started with initial equity of just ₹2.5 million, the capital grew to ₹375 million in financial year 2020–21, with the free reserves and a surplus of ₹5.04 billion! By 2020, the company had more than 600 branches across 18 states and union territories in India, employing about 4,500 people and servicing about 1.2 million active customers. Over the 10 years of its existence, Belstar had given a total credit of ₹120 billion![5]

My journey with Belstar is probably the most important one as it really solved the biggest challenge I had—sustainability for HIH and retention of staff. Handling a for-profit company was much easier than running a charity. As passionate as I am about HIH, it is Belstar that has given me the confidence for the second decade of HIH India. I transferred the best practices in human resources (HR), technology and productivity from Beltsar to HIH and also motivated several senior staff to provide their time pro bono to the NGO.

HAND IN HAND ACADEMY FOR SOCIAL ENTREPRENEURSHIP

'Never doubt that a small group of thoughtful, committed citizens can change the world; indeed, it's the only thing that ever has.'

—Margaret Mead

Right from the start, both Percy and I believed in sharing our expertise and experience to replicate the HIH model of job creation globally and the initial projects in Afghanistan, Brazil, South Africa and Cambodia confirmed that the model could be adapted and implemented in diverse contexts with appropriate modifications and capacity building of local populations. The initial idea was sending HIH employees to various countries and organizing training and hand-holding programmes as well as facilitating field visits to India. But this didn't seem like a feasible and sustainable solution.

As a part of my TRIUM Global Executive MBA (TRIUM EMBA), I had to prepare a capstone project with some of my classmates. After much deliberation, we chose the topic of setting up an academy for social entrepreneurship for HIH. The rationale was that a permanent institution with a regular set of trainers and academicians would be a more effective platform to disseminate knowledge and facilitate learning. I had already established connections with the HBS, the Stockholm School of Economics, Indian Institute of Management (IIM) Bangalore and IIT Madras.

Even within India, the huge number of women entrepreneurs nurtured by HIH provided a captive audience for advanced programmes; these women could also serve as motivators for future leaders. Thus was born the Hand in Hand Academy of Social Entrepreneurship, formally inaugurated in 2016 at Kaliyanoor village near Kanchipuram, although the first Global Social Entrepreneurship Programme was held in 2014.

I wanted the academy to have a distinct vibe, nestled amongst vibrant agricultural fields. We engaged a 'green builder' to construct a circular structure made of brick to keep the area cool throughout the year. We also placed a majestic Buddha statue in the middle so that the entire campus has a peaceful atmosphere. We implemented smart water conservation systems and developed a full-fledged canteen and dining area to cater to the needs of students from distant locations. I also ensured that the main lecture hall was dedicated to my mentor and named it Prof. Kash Rangan Auditorium.

The vision of the Academy was to cultivate entrepreneurs who would address social problems through sustainable enterprises. The academy hoped to do this through a mix of academic programmes designed to equip these passionate individuals with the tools and skills needed to create and successfully run socially relevant enterprises. In addition, Belstar Microfinance Limited needed to provide orientation for its new employees and offer refresher courses for regular staff to enhance and fine-tune their performances. It was also necessary for group entities to be exposed to the ethos of the organization and the values it stood for.

The Academy started offering certificate courses in banking, microfinance management, social entrepreneurship, housing finance, general insurance management, training courses for competitive exams for banks and financial institutions and English communication classes for employees. To improve the employability of the students, we partnered with the local Sri Chandrasekharendra Saraswathi Viswa Mahavidyalaya for our courses. The academy also signed an MOU with the Frankfurt School of Business to offer their part-time courses online.

Being situated in a remote village initially circumscribed the academy's reach but I managed to create one more institution that could continue the legacy of the HIH model through regular courses for both in-house and external candidates. The academy is now the home for learning and development activities of Belstar, fostering cross-learning amongst the different pillars and serving as a haven of learning for budding SHG entrepreneurs. By providing a platform for sharing the experiences of the thousands of women entrepreneurs nurtured by HIH since 2004 and the expertise of academicians and teachers, I felt that many more such enterprises would blossom across the world.

INDIAN NATURAL FARMERS PRODUCER COMPANY LIMITED

Agriculture in India has always been an integral part of its economy. At the time of independence of the country in 1947, more than 60 per cent of the population depended on agriculture and it accounted for a full 54 per cent of the GDP. Even though the share of agriculture in GDP has come down to 13 per cent, the population tied to agriculture has remained above 50 per cent. Small and marginal holdings of 2 hectares and less are a whopping 84 per cent of the holdings even after 70 years of independence![6]

The country tried many strategies like organizing agriculture cooperatives, SHGs, commodity interest groups, contract farming and farmer producer organizations to overcome the weaknesses of small holdings, the main one being the low levels of income and surplus to the majority of the farmers due to the asymmetry in marketing and pricing of inputs and output. Majority of the gains in farming went to the intermediaries and not to the primary producers. The other problem was the absence of processing and value addition. It was estimated that roughly a third of the produce was wasted in harvesting, transporting and storing. The farmers bore the brunt of this wastage of scarce resources and hard labour.

Based on the recommendations of an expert committee headed by Mr Y.K. Alagh, planning commission member, from 2002, the focus shifted to the farmer producer company or FPC formed under the existing Companies Act, combining the advantages of a farmer cooperative with the operational flexibility and efficiency of a private company. I felt this model to be a game changer for rural farmers and got to work.

HIH had been successfully implementing a number of watershed developments and Natural Resource Management (NRM) projects mainly funded by NABARD and other donors, gaining a fairly good experience in working with the farmers. Encouraged by NABARD, HIH's NRM pillar decided to form farmers' associations, focussing on organic farming, which was gaining traction in Tamil Nadu. The idea was to organize farmers into common interest groups, called organic farmers groups, at the district level. These groups would be unified into organic farmers associations, ensuring uniformity in practices and marketing across Kanchipuram, Kadalur and Tiruvannamalai and the tribal hilly areas of Pachamalai in Tiruchirappalli and Jawadu hills in Vellore. In order to market the products under a common banner, the Indian Natural Farmers Producer Company Limited (INFPCL) was formed in 2014. The vision of INFPCL was 'promoting sustainable food production and making agriculture a profitable venture by processing, value addition and direct marketing of products'. The mission was to reach at least 15,000 farmers by 2025. In 2021, INFPCL ventured into online marketing and introduced a brand 'Bhumi Pride', having a turnover of ₹30 million by the year 2019–20.[7]

By 2021, INFPCL had 3,200 organic farmers in its district associations and 7,200 farmers selling their produce to the company. The product range included grains of many varieties, pulses, millets and millet products, oil and ghee, spices and honey. The company also set up processing units in Kanchipuram and Jawadu hills to clean and grade the grains and make value-added products like health mixes and flour for making dosas.

MAHATMA GANDHI EDUCATIONAL TRUST

Since its inception, HIH's primary objective was to enrol and reintegrate children back into school. Before I joined, this was done through Olle School, which was more of an institution where students from the weaving community would work in the morning and attend classes in the evening. The school also focussed on tribal children, with 16 out of 116 students in its first year belonging to tribal communities.

Upon joining HIH, I realized that this model was not sustainable. An adult who works throughout the day will be tired and not have the energy in the evening to pursue learning activities; similarly, children will too feel the same and this needed to be respected. It is the right of the child to enjoy their childhood and attend school. Evening schools were not a long-term solution but only a temporary measure for imparting knowledge to exhausted children.

With the help of Dr Mangala Ayre, I established a new institution—a full-time school focussing on the children of weavers and tribal communities in and around Kanchipuram. The Mahatma Gandhi Educational Trust was thus set up, which has grown from one to two institutions over a period of 15 years. The first school is in Kanchipuram and the second is just 15 minutes away in Kaliyanoor. As of 2023, 1,100 students are enrolled, receiving high-quality education with excellent infrastructure facilities.

HAND IN HAND SWTIZERLAND

Through my first 10 years with HIH, I had numerous opportunities to discuss our impactful work with different stakeholders—the government representatives, private companies, heads of different countries, large international organizations and philanthropists. I knew that no one could talk about our work better than me and my team as we were the ones working directly with the communities day in and day out. To have an understanding of global fundraising trends and to liaise with potential international donors, I did the unthinkable—I set up a fundraising organization in Switzerland in 2013 to support the projects of HIH in India, Cambodia, Myanmar and Sri Lanka.

My colleague, Mr Sandip Mookerjee, has been a pillar of strength in institutionalizing this organization as it involves dealing with Swiss regulations and laws. We chose Geneva as it is the home of the UN. To strengthen our Board, we onboarded Mr Amitava Tripathi, former Indian Ambassador to Switzerland, as the advisor in our General Assembly, along with other eminent personalities. The initial years were particularly challenging, both from a statutory perspective and in establishing a trustworthy name for us amongst the 750 NGOs set up in Geneva at that time.[8]

With different sets of colleagues, I have visited Switzerland at least 20 times. My days were packed with meetings with foundations and philanthropists, arranged through friends and colleagues. These meetings—often long and conducted over cups of coffee and sandwiches—provided opportunities to showcase our work and catch the interest of donors. I always played a small video or film about our projects to give the donors a real sense of what we do. This approach helped me connect with them. Our first breakthrough was from Humanim, an NGO run by Arndt and Olivier Soret that focusses on children's rights. They supported our Village Uplift Programmes in 2013 and continue to do so.

Fund raising is an art that requires a lot of patience and the ability to accept rejections with grace. We modified our approach and simplified our five pillars to just three: Education, Empowerment and Environment, and renamed VUP to 'Dream Village'.

To further consolidate our local presence, we started hosting events in Geneva, using Hand in Hand Switzerland as a platform for knowledge sharing and information dissemination. Over time and with the support of our colleagues, we achieved major breakthroughs with large foundations. Today, the balance sheet of HIH Switzerland sits at almost Swiss franc (CHF) 2,50,000. The organization has received funds from the City of Geneva, marking our presence in the beautiful country for close to a decade.

VARASHAKTI HOUSING FINANCE

In my 20 years of work experience running both a for-profit and a not-for-profit, HIH's work gives me immense joy but Belstar's success gives me profound pride. I say this because Belstar operates as a socially conscious MFI and its growth has provided sustainability for HIH and the other institutions mentioned in this chapter.

Through Belstar's journey, I noticed a gap in the affordable housing finance space in rural India. As an NBFC-MFI, Belstar had its limitations in lending for housing purposes. To address this, I established Varashakti Housing Finance, an affordable housing finance company, in 2017. It has since grown to reach an assets under management of ₹190 crores and extending loans to 5,585 clients. Varashakti Housing Finance is professionally managed by a separate team and Board of Directors.

SEED TRUST

Getting foreign funds into an Indian NGO necessitates having a Foreign Contributions Regulations Act Licence from the Ministry of Home Affairs, Government of India. During HIH India's early days, while the organization was in the process of obtaining this, donors from Sweden expressed keen interest in supporting our projects. I didn't want to lose any opportunity to help the communities and in 2004, I acquired a dormant trust that already had a licence.

The Socio Economic and Educational Development (SEED) Trust had a clear vision and mission that aligned with HIH's objectives. Similar to HIH, SEED aimed to uplift individuals at the bottom of the socioeconomic pyramid, striving to create a sustainable and replicable poverty reduction model. My quick acquisition of SEED Trust was a timely help in the early days as it ensured funding for projects and maintaining the staffing structure transparently. It also gave me and my team the confidence to develop new project initiatives with long-term objectives. The trust remains operational, continuing its efforts in social security awareness, village uplift programmes and health initiatives.

HELPING HANDS TRUST

In 2008, we were approached by some donors abroad who expressed keen interest in some products crafted by our

SHGs. These included small handicrafts, artefacts, bags and dolls. I knew this would be a huge marketing opportunity for these women as long as they met the quality and quantity demands of the international market. I wanted to help the entrepreneurs thrive and set up the Helping Hands Trust, with its main focus being the promotion of export opportunities for the women of the SHGs and their enterprises. Some of the industries they worked in were tailoring, candle-making and bag-making. Notably, a huge consignment of teddy bears was exported to Bo Bear, a Swedish company, which marked a significant achievement for these women! The trust continues to work for its mission and now also supports in marketing farmers' products under the brand name 'Bhumi Pride'.

~

As the regulatory framework grew increasingly complex over the years, leaving very little time for strategizing and planning, maintaining the non-negotiables and high standards of the organization also became challenging. At times, I found myself questioning whether my struggles were worth all the effort. The only solace was the smiles I could see now and then on the faces of the thousands whose lives I could brighten over the years.

Top: Me as a baby at my first home in Pallavaram, Chennai
Bottom: With my parents and sisters at Rishikesh, circa 1976

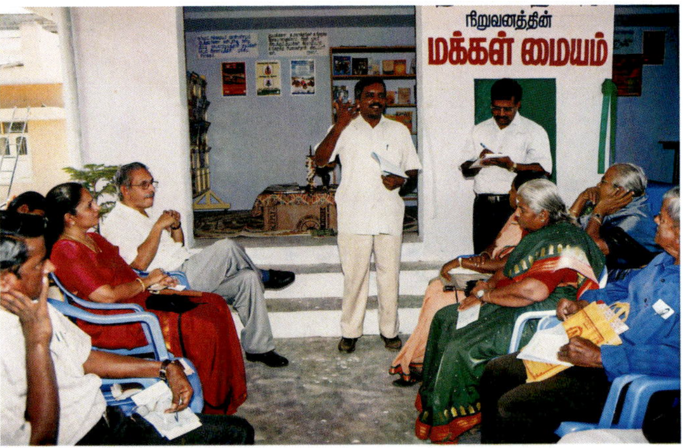

Top: Percy and I at one of our first self-help group (SHG) meetings in late 2004
Middle: With our first batch of graduates from the Poongavanam Residential Special Training Centre in 2006
Bottom: Inauguration of our first Citizens' Centre in 2005

Top: A SHG meeting in Cambodia in 2016
Middle: With Ms Ela Gandhi, granddaughter of Mahatma Gandhi, in South Africa in 2006
Bottom: With delegates from South Africa at a traditional silk weaving loom in Kanchipuram in 2005

INTER-AMERICAN DEVELOPMENT BANK
WASHINGTON, D.C. 20577

PRESIDENT

November 30, 2010

Dr. Kalpana Sankar
CEO and Managing Trustee
Hand in Hand
Tamil Nadu, India

Dear Dr. Sankar:

It was a great pleasure to meet you during my recent visit to India, on the occasion of the World Economic Forum. I sincerely appreciate the time we had to exchange views on the main issues affecting the development in Latin America and the Caribbean countries, as well as to discuss the opportunities that the region offers for the Indian private sector.

It is in no small measure thanks to the cooperation of devoted organizations such as Hand in Hand that we are able to, as you very well mentioned, touch the lives of so many in the Latin American and Caribbean Region.

I look forward to meeting with you in the near future and for a continued cooperation between our organizations for the years to come,

Sincerely,

Luis Alberto Moreno

Top: Training and scoping study with my team in Brazil in 2008
Bottom: Letter from Luis Alberto Moreno, President of the Inter-American Development Bank, applauding our work in Brazil

د کلیو د بیا رغونې او پراختیا وزارت
وزارت احیا و انکشاف دهات

د افغانستان اسلامي جمهوریت
جمهوری اسلامی افغانستان

Islamic Republic of Afghanistan
Ministry of Rural Rehabilitation & Development

شماره:
تاریخ:

Mr. Akhilesh Mishra
Deputy Chief of Mission
Embassy of India
Kabul, Afghanistan.

June 16, 2009

Dear Mr. Mishra,

<u>Information on MRRD's Rural Enterprise Development Program</u>

It is my pleasure to herewith present you with an informational CD containing material about the objectives, rationale and strategy of Afghanistan Rural Enterprise Development Program (AREDP) of the Ministry of Rural Rehabilitation and Development (MRRD.)

AREDP is this ministry's latest developmental undertaking and is aimed at creating sustainable employment opportunities for men and women across rural Afghanistan. As you are aware, a pilot of this program is already being implemented by Hand-in-Hand with generous funding from the Indian Government in two districts of Balkh province. This pilot has provided a number of lessons learnt that have been incorporated in the design of the main AREDP program.

I take this opportunity to thank the Government of India for its tireless efforts in the reconstruction and development of Afghanistan.

Yours Sincerely,

Wais Ahmad Barmak
Deputy Minister for Program

Top: A women's SHG meeting in Afghanistan in 2008
Bottom: Letter from the Ministry of Rural Rehabilitation and Development, Afghanistan, acknowledging our work

Top: With Mr Richard Verma, former US Ambassador to India, at a women's SHG meeting in Kanchipuram

Bottom: My family and I are ardent devotees of Sathya Sai Baba and we inaugurated a tele centre for the visually impaired in partnership with the Sri Sathya Sai Seva Organization in 2024

Top: With Matt Damon and Gary White, co-founders of Water.org, at Kanchipuram in 2012
Middle: Sahaana and I with Muhammad Yunus, father of microfinance, in Chennai
Bottom: With Percy Barnevik, Charlotte Bohman and Sahaana in Stockholm in 2017

Top: Signing the term sheet with Mr Lars Thunnel of the International Finance Corporation for their investment in Belstar in 2009
Middle: Prof Kash Rangan of Harvard Business School inaugurating our Hand in Hand Academy for Social Entrepreneurship campus at Kaliyanoor, Kanchipuram in 2016
Bottom: With Mr George Alexander Muthoot, Managing Director of Muthoot Finance, at a skill development centre run by Hand in Hand India

Top: Presenting Hand in Hand's work at Papua New Guinea in 2013
Bottom: Representing India at the G20 meet held in Hawaii in 2017

Top: Receiving the Nari Shakti Puraskar in 2017 from Shri Pranab Mukherjee, former President of India, for my work towards women's empowerment

Bottom: Receiving the Pradhan Mantri Bal Kalyan Puraskar from the President of India, Shri Ramnath Kovind, on behalf of Hand in Hand India for our child welfare initiatives in January 2019

Top: Meeting Prime Minister Narendra Modi at his residence in 2019
Bottom: Receiving the Global Award for Women's Empowerment at the United Nations Headquarters in New York in March 2019

Top: Receiving the Lifetime Achievement Award by ACCESS and Ministry of Finance, Government of India, in 2023 for my work towards financial inclusion

Bottom: With my TRIUM cohort in New York. I'm right in the middle, second row from the top

Top: With the Board of Directors of Belstar Microfinance Limited
Bottom: With the Board of Trustees of Hand in Hand India

Top: Celebrating 10 years of Hand in Hand India with some of our child labour elimination programme alumni

Bottom: Celebrating 20 years of Hand in Hand India with senior team members and Trustees

Top: With my husband, Sankar, and daughter, Sahaana
Bottom: At my dearest granddaughter Samaira's naming ceremony in 2022

Top: With some of the most important women in my life—my mother, Vijayalakshmi, and my sisters, Bindu and Kamini
Bottom: My sisters and their families during Sahaana and Srashta's wedding

7

SHARPENING THE SAW

'We must never become too busy sawing to take time to sharpen the saw.'

—Stephen Covey

From the very beginning, I wanted to broaden my horizons by expanding my social circle. I intended to spend time with diverse people and cultures to enrich myself and share my work with them for an effective peer review. At the same time, I realized that in order to maintain the organization, I needed to reinvent our model to generate new ideas and solutions. I needed to make meaningful connections with other people involved in similar activities. This could only happen with me going back to school and sharpen my saw. Thus, began a brand-new journey for me which had a profound impact on my life.

My first foray into international training within a formal academic setup started with the INSEAD Social

Entrepreneurship Programme at Institut Européen d'Administration des Affaires (INSEAD), Fountainbleu, France in December 2007. The course was intensive, focussing on leadership, team building, leading by example and the establishment and management of social enterprises.

At INSEAD, I was the only one in a cohort of 20 who was a mother! Observing the lives of people in the West, especially women, was eye-opening. They were fierce and independent, comfortable living their lives on their own terms without worrying too much about social expectations. Many had chosen not to have children in order to pursue their ambitions. Their thought process was intriguing for me and contributed to my growth in understanding the world from a global perspective. This course helped me foster an inclusive and empathetic attitude towards everyone.

One particular module on leadership and teamwork at INSEAD left a lasting impression on me. We were shown a video of a group of mountaineers conquering Mount Everest despite all odds. This video resonated deeply with me, prompting reflection on my journey with HIH. It became apparent that our organization needed to transition from an 'I' to 'we' mindset. It threw light on HR principles and the importance of grooming the team and giving them opportunities, emphasizing the importance of effective team management, resource allocation, motivation, strategic planning and execution, perseverance and most importantly, thinking on one's feet, especially at crucial times of crisis. Just as only one group of mountaineers successfully reached the summit in the video, I realized the critical role of leadership in guiding my team to success. This insight underscored the need for me to impart the knowledge and experiences gained from programmes like INSEAD to my team, fostering a culture of continuous learning and growth within the organization.

❧

Attending the course on the New Paradigms in Microfinance at the Boulder Institute of Microfinance in Turin, Italy, in July–August 2008 resulted in a paradigm shift in my thinking in terms of making the HIH model sustainable. The course content was extensive, covering a range of topics including new microcredit methodologies, financial analysis of microfinance companies, product diversification, risk management, fraud detection, microfinance funding, microinsurance, community-managed microfinance, transformation of microfinance companies and legally managing such transformation and Islamic microfinance. While most leaders of not-for-profits have a background in sociology, statistics or economics, this course reiterated the importance of management training in effectively running a social enterprise.

Not-for-profit organizations and microfinance companies were encountering regulatory roadblocks as getting capital from foreign donors involved a cumbersome process and local banks, after initial enthusiasm, waited for new equity before providing loans. There was also the danger of the NGO not being able to fund its microfinance activities that would help it to cross subsidize its core activities like child labour elimination, health initiatives and good governance programmes. There was a limit to the recycling of loan repayments and retention of high-quality staff would be difficult without continuous expansion.

The teachers at Boulder presented case studies of successful microfinance companies that achieved profitability with just 5,000 clients and how 90 per cent NGOs failed in their efforts to transition from socially relevant but intrinsically unsustainable operations to profit-making entities that remained true to their core objectives.

The training at Turin opened my eyes to the key point that donor money will not last for ever and I needed a sustainability plan. For this, I needed to create institutions that work for profit but with a social cause. One of my immediate key takeaways was the necessity of investing in systems, senior management, and gaining buy-in from NGO founders and staff to successfully navigate the transformation process.

This training came at a very critical juncture for HIH and me, following the explosive growth spearheaded by me since 2004. Percy noted later that HIH took off like a rocket after I joined!

The insights gained from the Boulder training helped me chart the way forward. I devised a plan where the core NGO, HIH, would remain a trust, continuing its partly sustainable activities across all pillars while also focussing on skill building and training of SHGs and providing their initial funding; the not-for-profit company would expand the credit activities, using its profits to support the NGO's unsustainable activities. Additionally, an NBFC would be established or acquired to undertake microfinancing as a purely commercial activity, enabling matured SHGs access more funds and grow into small and medium-scale enterprises, eventually gaining access to bank credit.

This transformation also entailed continuous mentoring of all the staff, especially at the senior levels, to ensure that the market-driven model did not compromise the core principles of working for the betterment of the poor. I also decided to take strategic decisions based not only on the bottom line but also on the impact these would have on the lives of the underprivileged.

I initiated microfinance operations through an existing NBFC, which had the license from the regulator, as the process of registering a new NBFC was getting delayed and raising capital in India was a challenge; using foreign funds for the same was not an option.

The Boulder training had in fact made me 'bolder'!

~

By early 2009, HIH India had assisted about 4,00,000 women through its own funds and those from other financial institutions within just four years—a feat that would typically require at least 10–15 years. However, to sustain this growth, a paradigm shift was required to obtain funds and not lose on the core people-centric operations of assisting families come out of the poverty trap while maintaining high quality and integrity.[1]

I attended a programme on Strategic Leadership for Microfinance at HBS sponsored by the HBS-Accion in April 2009. This programme introduced me to Prof. Kash Rangan and Prof. Michael Chu, acknowledged experts in microfinance and social entrepreneurship.

My objective was clear: I needed a strategy to propel HIH to the next level, one that could meet the credit needs of the thousands of women organized into SHGs. I needed to rally 2,800 full-time and 3,500 part-time employees along with me while continuing our work across other pillars. I was looking forward to this challenge!

~

The HBS programme helped me refine my strategies and learn from the pitfalls and experiences of other NGOs. I consider Prof. Kash my mentor as his classes blew my mind. In the famed halls of HBS, he ensured we all shed our ego by emphasizing that the biggest trait one requires as a social entrepreneur is sensitivity. We need to be sensitive and thoughtful when we work with people occupying the bottom of the pyramid. He walked us through the chilling Andhra Pradesh MFI crisis,[2] delving deep into what led to it and how MFIs could avoid such a situation.

This experience gave me a clear perspective on how I wanted to run my MFI, Belstar, in a socially responsible way. This ethic remains to date, from the senior team to the field team.

It was at the HBS-Accion programme that I met Ms Padmaja Reddy of Spandana, a large Indian MFI. Meeting her gave me the confidence that I too can scale my work with the right approach. Prof. Kash Rangan continues to be associated with us through many of the global social entrepreneurship programmes organized by HIH India.

~

Before joining HIH I had evaluated a number of projects for the United Nations Office for Project Services, United Nations Development Programme, Christian Aid and Wetlands International. My experience as a research associate at the Institute of Mathematical Sciences, Chennai, and later as a PhD scholar at Madras University had also provided me with a unique analytical perspective, allowing me to assess the progress of any work using clear metrics and mathematical tools. These qualifications helped me to quickly grasp the crux of the issues and strategize for any given situation.

Working with Percy further sharpened these skills, adding a focus on budgets, funding and value addition, with a clear focus on outcomes. Percy always used to say, 'Anything that gets measured, gets done.' For example, Percy and I would not merely monitor the number of out-of-school children mainstreamed into government schools but also consider how many of them cleared the 10th-grade board exams, which is critical for further education and employment. Similarly, we would not just focus on the number of loans given to the women but on the number of new enterprises started and jobs created. This kind of rigorous evaluation and decision-making was new in the NGO sector, which was more driven by lofty principles and commitment and unsustainable without constant outside support.

The model Percy and I developed was aimed at empowering families, students and the village people become prosperous and lead meaningful lives. An IIT Madras study later revealed that the social return on investment (SROI) of every rupee spent by HIH was actually ₹42![3]

Percy also taught me the importance of presentation and marketing. Just doing impactful work is not enough; it needs to be presented to an external audience. His perspective on the annual reports and websites is something I ensure to carry forward to date.

The training from HBS was insightful but took a while to put in perspective. While I endeavoured to ensure continuous donor funding, the team continued to do impactful work.

~

In August–September 2009, the East-West Center at Honolulu, Hawaii, invited me to participate in the Changing Faces Women's Leadership Seminar. Women who have created or run huge economic enterprises from all over the world speak about their experiences and challenges in this seminar.

This experience is very close to my heart as I was the only Indian selected for this programme. Travelling to the small but beautiful American island in the Pacific Ocean was an adventure in itself!

What made the experience even more special was the fact that it was an all-women cohort. I found strength and solidarity among this diverse group of women, who were in different stages of growth of their enterprises; it was a valuable learning experience. The programme allowed me the opportunity to prepare a 6-month action plan and structure my thoughts.

The moment of pride was being felicitated by the United State Congress at the end of the programme. Hawaii was also a place that I fell in love with and would go back to few times as a guest of the East-West Center.

ꟷ

The story of HIH has been the subject of several case studies. One of the first case studies was done by Lin Lerpold, Assistant Professor at the Stockholm School of Economics, along with Professor Harry Barkema from the Rotterdam School of Management and LSE and Anders Sjoman from Springtime Communications in October 2008.[4]

The year 2008 was critical for HIH's story as I faced the dilemma of sustaining the rapid growth of the last four years while maintaining high quality across diverse activities. Unlike traditional non-profits that focussed on a specific area of activity like education, health or advocacy for disadvantaged groups of people, HIH had dared to venture in diverse fields like child labour elimination, enterprise and job creation and environment initiatives while ensuring to employ people who displayed integrity and professionalism. This was an interesting aspect kindling the interest of students and management teachers alike.

My establishment of a for-profit microfinance company in 2008 became the subject of case study for Prof. M.S. Sriram from IIM Bangalore,[5] and for research scholars at the Stanford Graduate School of Business like Annie Adams, Lyn Denend, Sarah Garrett, Whit Keuer and Garth Saloner.[6] They studied the inherent conflict between building a sustainable organization capable of scaling its operations to reach more people while continuing to provide personalized pro bono development services that had driven the organization's growth thus far.

While I was grateful for Percy's support, I was anxious to avoid the challenges associated with depending on a single large donor; the task was to strike a balance in pricing some of the services and cross-subsidizing the inherently difficult areas.

❧

In 2001, the New York University (NYU) Stern School of Business, LSE and the HEC Paris collaborated to launch the TRIUM Global EMBA programme designed to address the global strategic challenges facing 21st century leaders. The programme drew mid-career executives from more than 75 countries in the first 10 years.

As part of the social entrepreneurship class, Professor Harry Barkema's case study conducted in the year 2008 on HIH was taught a part of the TRIUM curriculum. I was invited to New Delhi in 2009 to defend this case to the TRIUM cohort who had come to attend a module in the city. This was a unique experience for me, standing alongside a distinguished professor on the other side of the classroom!

Harry led the class through the study and let me take the questions from the students. These were not just any students but 65 CEOs or COOs from leading corporates who posed pertinent questions on sustainability, challenges, global replication and financing. It also allowed me to go home and reflect deeply on how we can improve our work at HIH.

My performance was so well received that the dean of the programme, Mary Logan, decided to shift the programme in India to Chennai so that the students could visit HIH at Kanchipuram. This was a very special moment for me and the students as they got the practical exposure through field visits. From 2010, this programme continued till 2017 with about 70–90 students and faculty visiting Kanchipuram every year. Hosting the TRIUM cohort for close to eight years also brought me closer to Mary.

In 2010, I was offered a scholarship to join the TRIUM programme and became part of the Class of 2012, travelling across UK, France, USA, China and India. This programme was one of the most important education experiences for me as it provided rigorous training in management areas like strategy, risk assessment, financial ratios and analysis, brand building, leadership, negotiation skills, technology and human resources management. My classmates came from diverse backgrounds, with some even using private planes to attend the classes at different locations. Many of them held senior positions in multinationals.

The first term was at the prestigious LSE during autumn. I was extremely impressed and inspired by how hard they worked, how efficiently they managed their time, how thorough their preparation was before any session and how actively they participated in the group work. The coursework was intensive, with leaders of the International Monetary Fund and World Bank providing insights into the global economy. This was starkly different from the one-dimensional blackboard to textbook approach followed in the classrooms of India that I was used to and it took quite some time for me to adjust. I can only say that I emerged from the programme with rich and varied experiences.

I distinctly remember a day when I decided to take a detour from my usual routine. I was a diligent student who usually attended classes regularly; that day, I decided to take some time off to relax as I was exhausted. I skipped my morning classes and went shopping, hoping to enjoy the day but the Dean sent me a strict letter in the afternoon, stating that I would not get my certificate if I missed }another session. I felt extremely guilty and promised never to skip any sessions, doubling my efforts to excel academically.

~

What makes the TRIUM EMBA different is the balanced exposure to the three prestigious universities and the developing nations as well. During the course, one exposure visit was to India, which HIH hosted, and the other was to China.

Before my trip to China as a part of the TRIUM programme, I had visited Kunming in 2008 to evaluate whether the HIH job creation model could be replicated there. Though there was abject poverty alongside rapidly developing infrastructure, there was no scope for project replication owing to a complex civil society working environment that was under the watchful eyes of the government.

My visit to Shanghai for the TRIUM course in 2010 was starkly different! The city seemed like an Asian San Francisco—tall buildings, booming IT, thriving finance crowd and even Indian restaurants. The coursework too was interesting.

∽

In January 2011, a snowy New York welcomed me for my second term at the NYU Stern School of Business. The city looked absolutely stunning with remnants of Christmas lights adorning the high-rises. Often called 'mean London,' New York lived up to its reputation. When I caught the taxi to go to the university campus and paid the driver the exact amount, he flung the notes back at me—I did not know I needed to tip him at least 10 per cent. What a rude shock it was!

The −5°C temperature was also something I was not prepared for. The snow was thick and turned into sheets of ice a day after fresh snowfall. A helpful classmate guided me to Bloomingdales on 5th Avenue to get a suitable winter jacket. There, a friendly Bangladeshi salesperson found me the perfect jacket for $800!

I spent close to half of my money on this but I could not have survived the two-week course without it. The classes were extremely invigorating and interesting. Though I was used to working with Excel sheets data for impact evaluation during my government job days, this was the first time I had to work on financial ratios with 400 excel sheet rows. After classes, I would explore the bustling city of New York that literally never sleeps.

Under the guidance of Prof. Aswath Damodaran, the valuation guru, I was able to take a deep dive into finance and accounting like never before. At the end of his session, we all stood up to give him a standing ovation. It was also a proud moment for me as an Indian, to learn from professors like him and Sonia Maricano, who taught corporate strategy. Prof. Aswath's sound concepts have helped me to date, especially dealing with the growing Belstar that is on its way to an Initial Public Offering (IPO)!

~

Before concluding the programme in London, we spent a term at the beautiful campus of HEC near Paris, which turned out to be the most enjoyable. The course content focussed on luxury and marketing—areas I didn't relate to but found intriguing. It underscored how we can create a niche for ourselves and be a differentiator. A visit to the luxury giant Louis Vuitton's factory is something I can never forget!

The term in Paris was like paradise as by then, I was acclimatized to the TRIUM cohort and schedules. I was well prepared and enjoyed gourmet food and drinks after my classes!

My active involvement and commitment encouraged the TRIUM programme organizers to offer similar scholarships to deserving students, especially from Asia and Africa, in the subsequent years. The classes were tough and I had to juggle my work in India till the last minute, rushing to classes in foreign locations, with no time for acclimatizing. Being a vegetarian, I could not always get the food I wanted and the colder climes proved particularly harsh. The subjects were new and complex and the students being mid-level executives could not expect any help from anyone, making it more strenuous. All this trouble was worth the while as it gave me an international degree and emboldened my confidence to break barriers and achieve the extraordinary.

∾

In November 2016, I attended a special programme on risk mitigation strategies and facing competition for the microfinance companies conducted by the International Finance Corporation (IFC) at New York. I was sponsored by the Small Industries Development Bank of India (SIDBI) as by this time, both HIH and Belstar Microfinance Limited had many graduated clients who had transitioned into micro and small-scale businesses.

My key takeaways from this programme were the importance of having a risk department, adhering to global standards of measurement and best practices. Learning about the challenges faced by other organizations and how they overcame was particularly enlightening. IFC is a mecca for investments and the short course was intense, with senior faculty providing highly valuable insights. Upon returning to India, I documented the best practices as a booklet and gave it to SIDBI.

∾

My background in pure science, coupled with my experience in monitoring and evaluating internationally funded projects, provided me with a sound foundation in project appraisals and strategy refinement. It has enabled me to discern what strategies and approaches would work where, evaluate performances against agreed benchmarks and make necessary modifications to the programme content and delivery.

My interactions with Percy helped me understand how to budget for deliverables and think big. Percy's initial funding and guidance helped me focus my energies on fine-tuning the programmes without compromising on quality due to cost-cutting and engaging better-quality personnel. I was able to deliver high-quality programmes without cost or time overruns.

While the Boulder course helped me to look at long-term sustainability by cross-subsidizing the not-for-profit operations through microfinance, the courses at HBS-Accion and IFC helped me understand the contemporary global developments and think ahead. The TRIUM course broadened my perspective on what attracts international business leaders, helping me grow beyond my socially motivated thought process and giving me the confidence to negotiate successfully with large-scale foundations and enterprises.

Continuous interactions with interns from institutions like the Stockholm School of Economics, LSE, Stanford University, IIM Bangalore, and later from TRIUM, kept me and my team on our toes with fresh insights. The students brought a new perspective in the model and their enthusiasm energized us to reach for greater goals and impact.

My global experiences have reinforced the fact that women are at a disadvantage because of social conditioning, mental conditioning and the lack of opportunities. Despite legal provisions granting women equal rights, the representation of women-led businesses in India remains at a mere 14 per cent.[7] India now mandates that there should be at least one woman on the board of directors of any company as per the second clause in Section 149(1) of the Companies Act, 2013.[8] This one woman can bring such a different perspective especially for companies dealing with products consumed by women. Imagine how an equally represented board would look like. Including women at all levels at decision-making on par with men remains a distant dream.

The challenges women face in their careers, particularly due to the constraints of the biological, often stalls their progression to senior levels. Few women have the necessary family support and resilience to navigate this phase and rise. Fostering a conducive work environment and implementing supportive policies can help bridge this divide. Other than my East-West Center cohort that was all women, our representation at the senior levels remains below 37 per cent.[9]

I strongly believe that education plays a crucial role in bridging gender disparities. However, it is the exposure one gets from interacting with global peers and experiencing their culture that fosters holistic development. With each course I attended, I could feel my confidence surge as I witnessed myself transforming into a successful female entrepreneur!

8

THE FIVE PILLARS OF HAND IN HAND

'Poverty is the worst form of violence.'

—Mahatma Gandhi

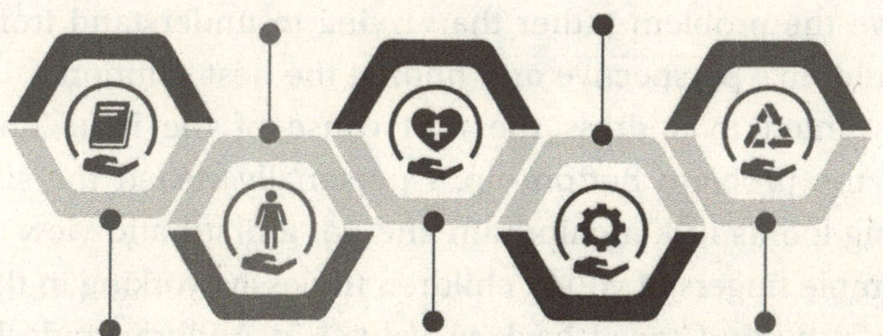

CHILDHOOD REGAINED: THE CHILD LABOUR ELIMINATION PROGRAMME

When I worked on a project funded by the World Bank as part of the Government of Tamil Nadu, I had the opportunity to visit the Velugu Project in Andhra Pradesh. They operated a residential centre for children who were employed as labourers in the cotton fields. Cotton picking was a strenuous task and the residential centre proved to be a blessing for them.

When I joined HIH, the primary programme the organization was running was the CLEP. The existing programme was purely focussed on weaning away the child labourers by securing their release from their employers and reintegrating them into schools. This approach had very limited success as it didn't address the root cause of poverty beyond providing some food materials to the families. Children who had never been to school were not motivated enough to consider education as their pathway out of abject poverty. Moreover, the cash payments made to the employers only encouraged more child labourers surfacing to benefit from the generosity of the foreigners. Even the government programmes focussed on after-work schools, clearly bypassing the onerous task of removing the children from labour altogether. Everyone was looking for an intervention to solve the problem rather than trying to understand from the children's perspective and finding the best solution.

I wanted to address the root cause of the issue and tackle the problem bottom-up. I personally visited the silk weaving looms in Kanchipuram and got a first-hand view of the nimble fingers of young children tirelessly working in the looms; my mind raced back to Velugu in Andhra Pradesh. It became clear that that establishing a residential centre for these children would be the solution to restoring their lost childhood. I knew that I couldn't implement this alone and approached several NGOs and government institutions involved in this initiative. The learnings gained from them were essential in helping us solidify our model.

These NGOs had been working in this field for quite some time and had developed effective training and other methodologies and processes that could easily work in Tamil Nadu due to similarities in the backgrounds of affected children and societal conditions. They emphasized long-term transformation of the families of the children and the community through information and communication campaigns as a more sustainable approach than the short-term tactics of repayment of loans or official punitive measures and threats.[1]

We visited several institutions working to eradicate child labour and gleaned valuable insights from their approach and sought their help in implementing strategies, training volunteers and engaging with the communities.

In my first year, I came across a very moving incident involving a young girl named Sheela. Her fight for survival began when she was still inside her mother's womb. An unfortunate family feud had left her mother murdered and her father in jail. While the entire family thought little Sheela had died in her mother's womb, it was her grandmother's insistence on digging up the grave that revealed the newborn's miraculous survival.

Though she made a heroic comeback and got a second chance in life, her childhood was spent with her grandmother, receiving minimal care. At just eight years old, she found herself trapped as a child labourer in a small factory in Singadivakkam Village, Tamil Nadu, manufacturing rangoli powders. The intense sorrow in her intense eyes has still not left my memory. After listening to her story, I was convinced that our solution needed to combine compassion and care with learning and development.

I was particularly mindful of the teaching methodology as some of these children had never been exposed to formal education. My research led me to visit Isai Ambalam, a school in Auroville, Puducherry, which had successfully implemented an activity-based learning methodology ideal for children who had never attended school or had dropped out. Witnessing the enthusiasm with which the children were engaging in their studies promptly led us to implement the same approach at Kanchipuram. Sheela was enrolled in our Poongavanam RSTC and she successfully completed her 8th grade. She is currently employed in a private firm near Chennai and is married with two children.

The key for the success of this methodology that has impacted thousands of children like Sheela was the training of teachers. With activity-based learning becoming the norm in all state-run schools owing to the success of a pilot in Chennai's corporation schools,[2] the school run by HIH transitioned easily to the new system. The residential schools run for the bonded and child labourer children also adopted this method of teaching with great success. This exemplified my approach of leveraging the expertise of other organizations to further our objective of giving the best to the society.

The CLEP pillar of HIH encompassed a comprehensive approach to combat child labour. Starting with the RSTCs, the initiatives also included transit centres for tutoring students who had failed their examinations, providing support to the government schools with extra teachers and aids, assistance in the repair and renovation of school classrooms and libraries and operating satellite centres during challenging times such as the COVID-19 pandemic. The CLEP was the first major initiative of HIH and served as the organization's the entry point to all the villages where it operated.

More than 1,200 Child Labour Free Panchayats were created with the active support of local political leaders and community members; Child Welfare Committees were also formed to sustain focus on addressing child labour issues. By 2021, HIH had helped reintegrate more than 3,50,000 children into schools and restarted the educational journey of thousands of youngsters who had previously failed in a few of the subjects and had not been able to pass the school board exams.

The success of these initiatives can be attributed to the relentless efforts of our team, who engaged with and counselled local panchayat leaders, youth and SHG women, providing training on the rights of the children and right to education and why it was the community's responsibility to maintain schools and anganwadis.[3]

It was for these achievements that the Government of India felicitated the organization with the Pradhan Mantri Rashtriya Bal Kalyan Puraskar award in 2019.

EDUCATION—THE ONLY WEAPON TO CHANGE LIVES

MEERA: PROUD WINNER OF THE PRATHIBA AWARD

The first time I saw Meera was at the HIH office. Her smile was infectious and she had a medal around her neck. She held a certificate in her hand, with her proud parents standing beside her. Meera is one of the graduates of HIH's Dhamaneri RSTC. She was enrolled in the centre in 2013 after the HIH team spotted her doing odd jobs. Hailing from the marginalized Irular Community, her family's nomadic lifestyle meant they migrated every quarter. Meera and her three siblings helped their parents in their job, which included working in brick kilns, cutting wood in forests and tending to cattle. Owing to this lifestyle, Meera eventually dropped out of school.

Our team enrolled Meera and her three siblings at the RSTC, where she resumed her education from class six. After completing class eight, she was admitted to the Deenabandhu Trust-aided T.M. High School at the border of Tamil Nadu and Andhra Pradesh. Our team continuously monitored her progress to ensure she completed her 10th-grade board examination.

We were pleasantly surprised to hear that Meera had scored 78 per cent in the board examinations and secured the first position among ST students in Chittor mandal,[4] which earned her the 'Pratibha Award' from the Government of Andhra Pradesh. She is the first student from our HIH group to receive a state-level award and we are very proud of her.

The sad reality of poverty is that despite Meera's accolades and accomplishments and our constant motivation, her parents did not permit her to pursue further studies. Meera didn't complete higher education and chose to get married. She now lives in Sriperumputhur with her husband and seems to be happy. A world of potential could have been unlocked with her intelligence and hard work but Meera's case provides a reality check for me that despite our interventions and work, bringing about behavioural changes across generations remains a stiff challenge!

HANDS THAT WEAVE TO HANDS THAT TYPE!

At the tender age of nine, Suresh had to shoulder more responsibilities than any other child. He worked 12 hours a day in a weaving loom to support his family of four—his father, a flower garland vendor, his mother, a homemaker, and his two elder sisters.

In 2005, HIH India's mobilizers approached him and his family, advocating the importance of education and urging him to join Muthialpet Middle School. Bonded to the weaving loom for ₹2,000, HIH India facilitated a loan for Suresh and he was enrolled in class five.

To ensure that his education was not an additional burden for his family, Suresh continued to work part-time while he studied. HIH India's 'parcel scheme,' which provided basic kitchen and toiletry essentials to impoverished families, eased their financial strain. Alongside his studies and work, Suresh also coached students in throw ball, a sport he excelled at! He never wasted a single moment of his pre-adult life, always working to help uplift his family.

Suresh aced his 12th grade examination and enrolled for a Bachelors of Commerce degree in Pachaiyappa's College for Men, Kanchipuram on a scholarship. He attended classes during the day and worked as a data entry operator by night; he also honed his skills in typewriting and Tally software. He had realized at a very early age the importance of having a wide range of skills to succeed in a working environment.

Even before graduation, he had made up his mind to return to his alma mater, HIH India! When we asked how HIH India has changed his life, he claimed, 'Without HIH India, I won't even have had this shirt that I am wearing!'

Today, Suresh works as an accounts manager for HIH India's NRM team in Kanchipuram. He not only supports his parents but also ensures the continuation of his sisters' education.

Suresh's story highlights the cycle of life—a child labourer we had enrolled into school returns home to HIH as a colleague!

SELF-HELP IS THE BEST HELP: THE SELF-HELP WOMEN EMPOWERMENT PROGRAMME

As a Monitoring and Evaluation officer with the Women's Development Corporation, I started my work with the formulation of a project for poverty alleviation through the SHG movement, inspired by Prof. Yunus' work in Bangladesh. Piloting the formation of such groups made it clear that if child labour was to be tackled in a holistic and long-lasting manner, the only way was to economically empower the families through the leadership of women.

Though almost half of India's population comprises of women, their household work is largely ignored in any calculation of national income statistics. Despite considerable developments in education and opportunities, women are far from being equal to men in terms of prospects, benefits and power. Even today, there are pockets in India where female children are unwelcome and the practice of infanticide persists. To address these issues, the next pillar of HIH was established—SHGs of women who were in need of cash to start or improve their economic activities. Many of these women were illiterate and lacked knowledge of financial management, saving and banking. We implemented a systematic process to identify these women, train them using well thought out manuals, upskill them and support the formation of groups and foster group cohesion. Thousands of such groups were initially funded by HIH's own money and later bank credit and government subsidies were leveraged.

When HIH identified these SHGs as the vehicle for job creation and enterprise development, I got in touch with experts to design the orientation and capacity-building programmes for our staff and finding good trainers for the initiative.

Several NGOs already had a successful model for such groups and readily came on board. This collaboration helped us to scale up the programme quickly in its very first year. My confidence in roping in other agencies and institutions with expertise contributed to HIH's swift execution and high-quality delivery. This was possible due to a few reasons. Firstly, my past experience with the government had exposed me to some excellent grassroots organizations such as MYRADA, the Development of Humane Action (DHAN) Foundation, MVF, Isai Ambalam, Kalvi Kendra and Catalyst Trust—providing me with a wealth of knowledge and insights. Secondly, our initial board members from the CII connected us with relevant corporates in the early days. Thirdly, I never hesitated to ask for help, even from large foundations. For instance, Infosys Foundation was one of our earliest supporters; they donated brand new computers for our residential school children after a simple email request!

Percy appreciated the enthusiasm displayed by the SHGs in undertaking business activities and my ability to scale up quickly impressed him tremendously. The prompt repayment of loans by the SHGs generated more capital for lending and this cycle revolutionized the lives of hundreds of families. Right from the beginning, I ensured that the women not only received credit but were also advised on health, nutrition, environment, voting rights, the government schemes, veterinary care, finance and accounts and accessing technology.

Special apps were developed with donor support to encourage business-to-business marketing among the SHGs and members were provided regular training in entrepreneurship with the help of institutions like IIT Madras and the CII and the Federation of Indian Chambers of Commerce and Industry.[5] Cluster-level and block-level networks were formed to facilitate collaboration among members and improve their negotiation skills. Graduated clients with good credit records received increased support and were encouraged to start micro and small-scale enterprises. There were many instances where the husbands, on seeing the success of their wives, quit their jobs to help in the business.

SATHYA'S SOARING SUCCESS

One of our standout entrepreneurs is Sathya who had joined one of our SHGs as a housewife. In 2010, she grabbed the opportunity to take up a beauty and wellness training course at Green Trends, a popular salon that HIH India had an MOU with. Upon completing the course, she started her beauty practice from home. Within a short span of three years, her reputation as a skilled beautician spread across Kanchipuram. Further training sessions facilitated by Goldman Sachs through HIH India equipped her with crucial entrepreneurial skills such as time management, customer handling, and business development. She also recognized the importance of learning English and adopting an entrepreneurial attitude. Sathya's journey extended beyond personal success; she became a beautician trainer, empowering over 3,000 women. Remarkably, 97 of them, inspired by her guidance, established their own beauty parlours, becoming entrepreneurs themselves.

RATHIKA: THE RESILIENT ENTREPRENEUR

I met Rathika for the first time at an event where the HIH team had brought together successful women entrepreneurs. She was one of the five women sharing the stage with me to share their experiences. As she sat next to me, confident and smiling, I would have never imagined her life to so turbulent yet so successful. One of the 40 women from India to have been a part of the Goldman Sachs intensive business training programmes in partnership with the Indian School of Business, Rathika was a trailblazer!

Married at the young age of 14, Rathika had her first child at 15 and her next at 17. Though her husband encouraged her to pursue education, she knew the importance of financial stability for her family's future. Her first entrepreneurial venture was a small shop selling idli and dosa batter. Scaling this business proved to be a challenge and that is when she met my team at HIH India.

HIH provided her with essential resources, including a computer and printer, and equipped her with training and e-governance knowledge, enabling her to establish an e-service venture from her home. She knew that her future was in this field and enrolled as a business correspondent for the State Bank of India. In a short time, Rathika created a name for herself. She assisted young-old, male-female and literate-illiterate alike with a smile on her face. Through her services, she successfully assisted in opening 7,000 bank accounts and earned significant amounts through incentives. Additionally, she helped people with sourcing any documentation they needed through online services.

But life can throw a curveball at you at the most unexpected time. Tragedy struck when she lost her husband to kidney failure, resulting in emotional devastation and financial challenges. Nevertheless, Rathika displayed remarkable resilience, providing for her family, arranging her daughter's marriage and supporting her other child's career in medical coding. To enhance her career prospects, she took the courageous decision of resuming her education; she completed her schooling and diligently enhanced her knowledge and skills. Currently, Rathika operates an e-Seva Kendra and serves as a business correspondent for HDFC and Axis Banks, earning a stable income of around ₹25,000. Her journey as an entrepreneur has made her a role model in her community and she is affectionately referred to as 'Singappen' (Lion Lady), a testament to her strength and fortitude.

Rathika's story serves as a testament to the power of determination and resilience in the face of adversity, inspiring aspiring entrepreneurs, especially women, to overcome obstacles and achieve success in their entrepreneurial endeavours. Hearing her story moved me to tears and I couldn't help but be proud of my team who guided her in her journey!

TRANSFORMATION IN TURBULENT TIMES: TULSI BAI

The onset of COVID-19 in 2019 brought a lot of change and challenged for my team and me. The field staff were locked down and couldn't meet our beneficiaries and the transition to digital training took some time to settle down. We were in touch with our entrepreneurs and supported them where possible, training them on best practices in social distancing and safety precautions. Several of our women lost their jobs, depleted savings and even lost loved ones.

I came across Tulsi Devi's story when we were transitioning out of the first lockdown in phases. She had lost her husband to COVID-19 and was left to fend for her four children. Though she had previously received business training and microfinance loans from HIH, the sudden shock of losing her husband and the market difficulties posed a challenge to restart her business. Our team reached out to her and encouraged her to revive her bag-making unit once again by providing her with market linkages.

She bought old tailoring machines rather than new ones to minimize costs; her persistence and determination proved fruitful as her business got back on track over time. While her business picked up, Tulsi realized it was not enough and decided to start a tailoring training centre. This unit thrived and she also started getting orders from neighbouring locations, leading to the employment of six women from the SHGs.

Tulsi was a determined entrepreneur who learnt not only the art of tailoring but marketing, negotiation and pricing in a tough market. She broke patriarchal barriers of being a single woman and proved that entrepreneurship can thrive even when times are tough. Tulsi's story is an inspiration to me. Her grit and perseverance encourage us to continue our initiatives with vigour!

FEDERATIONS FOR THE FUTURE

Following the continued success of the SHG movement, the next step was federating groups of SHG women into CLN groups, each typically comprising 8–10 SHGs. These networks focus on advancing women's empowerment at the community level by addressing social, economic and political issues that are beyond the scope of individual SHGs.

Each CLN outlines a vision for their village or community and negotiates with local governments to implement simple but essential changes such as road construction, closure of local liquor shops or ensuring access to water. Some CLN members even hold positions as Panchayat Presidents! To consolidate these CLNs, block-level networks are formed with their own presidents and leaders to oversee the activities of the CLNs.

Since 2017, HIH has developed 2,636 CLNs with 2,66,942 members.[6]

Imagine what a trickle effect these groups of women can have in uplifting society!

❧

By December 2021, HIH and Belstar had formed 2,40,000 women's SHGs with a collective membership of 2.7 million. The credit disbursed was about ₹130 billion.[7]

A study on the SROI by IIT Madras revealed that the SHG programme yielded ₹42 for every ₹1 spent in formation, training and other parameters.[8] This study revealed that what could not be achieved through years of spending by the governments and financial institutions could be done in a sustainable way by trusting the impoverished, often uneducated women by supporting them when such help was most needed. The women realized that the success of their initiatives rested on their prompt repayment of the loans and worked accordingly. Political and other issues like corporate greed did indeed create difficulties in states like Andhra Pradesh but the quick remedial steps taken by the RBI and banks helped to calm the waters.[9]

Here, I am reminded of an entrepreneur from Afghanistan whose experience is etched in my memory. This Afghan woman had lost her husband to war and had no means for sustenance. We recognized her potential and provided her a $400 loan to start a tandoor bread-making venture. In six months, she was able to generate enough income to repay her loan and support her family.

ENVIRONMENT: SOLID WASTE AND NATURAL RESOURCE MANAGEMENT

Indian households typically generate about half a kilogram of solid waste per capita daily[10] and most of it can be recycled or used as biomass. Transport and treatment of this waste is a perennial problem for the local governments due to limited land and resources. Plastics and e-waste have added to the already existing mounds of garbage.

Mudichur is a small village in Kanchipuram district with about 7,000 households. The local Panchayat leader was looking for organizations that could help him to motivate people to keep the village clean. HIH stepped in to support his initiative in 2007.

I identified a few resource persons who had worked with ExNora, an organization that had established door-to-door segregation and processing of waste as the ideal cost-effective and environment-friendly method to reduce landfill waste. Leveraging the availability of labour at relatively lower costs, we advocated for waste segregation at the household instead of carrying mixed garbage to a distant landfill as about three-fourths of solid waste management costs were attributed to transportation of this garbage.

Instead of transporting mixed waste to the landfills and then separate it, our approach focussed on segregating waste at the source, enabling the recycling of paper, plastic, glass and composting of organic waste within households. I, along with my team of Green Friends, made door-to-door visits a simple affair. The panchayat provided a piece of land for a resource recovery park where items of marketable value were salvaged and either sold or recycled on-site.

From initially covering about 700 households, HIH

expanded its initiative to reach 6,800 households in the village. Recognizing the potential of food waste to produce biogas, which can fire a generator to produce electricity, HIH implemented a biogas generation system in Mahabalipuram, utilizing food waste to power street lights for free! As usual, HIH supplied labour and materials in advance to help the local bodies, who would reimburse the expenses later. The message and the work spread across many more local bodies and institutions like the Cantonment Board at Pallavaram, IIT Hyderabad, HCL Noida near Delhi and by December 2021, HIH's solid waste management team had covered 140 such establishments and about 6,40,000 households.[11]

The Green Friends were given PF and other facilities including loans for educating their children, enabling them to work in difficult conditions like floods, during COVID-19 etc. HIH created a successful model of sensitizing the households to segregate at source, employed local people as volunteers and Green Friends and set up a viable resource recovery park to reduce the burden on the landfills. Later, HIH added community safe drinking water reverse osmosis plants in more than 100 locations, e-waste handling and septage management to its repertoire. Its biggest project was in Karaikal, Puducherry, where it covered all 25,000 households, handling 40 tonnes of garbage daily!

WASTE WARRIORS: OUR GREEN FRIENDS

Our Green Friends are the true warriors of waste management. Take Muniyammal for instance. She joined HIH India as a Green Friend, serving on the frontline of the solid waste management project in Karaikal,

Puducherry. She is the sole breadwinner of her family as her husband has been unwell. Managing her family and working as a Green Friend tested her conviction. Despite her personal struggles, she ensured her children received the best education she could afford. Her daughter is currently an engineer working at an IT firm.

During the nationwide COVID-19 lockdown, understanding the need and defying all odds, Muniyammal led from the front in educating people on social distancing, hand washing and wearing masks while performing her primary task of waste collection at 250 households and exhorting people to practise segregation of waste at source.

A radio jockey from All India Radio, Karaikal station, once spotted Muniyammal and interviewed her during her awareness sessions, which made her the talk of the town. Impressed by her interview, an actor with social conscience, Anu Hasan, contacted and appreciated her for selfless contribution during the tough times of the COVID-19 pandemic. Their telephonic conversation, where Muniyammal shared her views on our environment and personal hygiene, went viral on social media.[12]

■

Andal, another Green Friend, was distraught when she lost her husband to alcoholism and had a debt of ₹5 lakh and three daughters to look after. Due to the discrimination these communities face in the country, finding a livelihood can prove to be a gruesome task. Andal started a small roadside eatery selling idlis but it was not sufficient to run the family. After seven years of running the eatery, she acquired a job in the housekeeping department in a reputed local hospital. She expected that a change in job would bring a change in fortune but the meagre salary of ₹4,000 per month was not even enough support her family's sustenance. Even worse was her 12-hour work schedule at the hospital that kept her away from her children for long periods. When HIH India recruited Green Friends for its 'Recycle for Life' project in Karaikal, Andal joined the project immediately. The salary offered was more than double, making her relaxed and happy. The 8-hour work schedule and the work ethics in the project were added bonuses, and she was finally able to spend quality time with her children. Two of her daughters are in college now and she has repaid most of her debt. In addition to that, she has helped 10 widows from her community, who all lost their husbands due to alcoholism, by recommending them for jobs as Green Friends in the project.

Muniyammal's and Andal's stories exemplify women's leadership as they both had to break through barriers to emerge as respected and thriving members of their societies!

❧

As part of its environment pillar activities, HIH started work in the micro watersheds in Arapedu village, Tamil Nadu in 2006 with support from NABARD. The work involved creating irrigation and drinking water ponds, soil treatment and improvement works, introducing new crop varieties, tree plantation and promoting organic and sustainable farm practices. The HIH team started working with tribal families in Karnataka in 2010 and branched into other states like Madhya Pradesh, taking advantage of corporate social responsibility funds. HIH introduced new crop varieties to farmers, such as papaya in Tamil Nadu and pepper in the Jawadhu Hills in Vellore.

By February 2022, the NRM projects of HIH totalled 140, covering multiple states in India including Madhya Pradesh, Gujarat and Haryana, besides Tamil Nadu. These projects treated about 33,000 hectares of land through various soil and water conservation measures, with about 6,000 hectares transitioning to organic farming. The HIH NRM team also built additional water storage capacity of about 4,27,000 cubic metre and planted close to 2.65 million fruit-bearing and other useful trees. True to the culture of HIH in nurturing communities, the team also mobilized community contributions of about ₹41 million, directly benefitting about 1,00,000 farmer families.[13]

The team adopted a holistic approach towards improving farm incomes by holding veterinary camps for farm animals besides introducing drip irrigation, solar panels for drying, hydroponics etc. to infuse new ideas among the farmer families. In many tribal areas, new varieties of flowers and other horticulture crops were introduced, which significantly increased farm incomes. The NRM initiative was clearly a successful venture of HIH facilitated by the cooperation and support of the state governments and NABARD.

Farmers with marginal landholdings are always on the edge of poverty and are most vulnerable to climate change, market volatility and have limited bargaining power in the agri-value chain. Since 2007, HIH India has been helping these farmers generate income through targeted interventions such as promoting crops that have high prices in the market, encouraging farmers to federate themselves through farmer producer companies and building a farm-to-fork retail chain to market high-quality organic produce. For these farmers, HIH India not only conducts training on latest agri-practices but also facilitates access to the government schemes. In addition, HIH undertakes soil enrichment programmes and invests in infrastructure development such as constructing bunds, check dams and renovation of water bodies.

In recent years, HIH has been working closely with tribal farmers across eight states in an effort to integrate these marginalized communities into the mainstream society. By June 2022, HIH had benefited 1,03,000 farmer families through its water harvesting and soil improvement initiatives and supported 26,000 farmers in producing and marketing organic produce.[14]

FARMERS PRODUCERS COMPANIES

At HIH, we have always been a friend of the farmer. With support from organizations such as NABARD, the National Cooperative Development Corporation, the Tribal Cooperative Marketing Development Federation and the National Stock Exchange, we have promoted 37 FPCs since 2014 towards facilitating backward and forward linkages for farmers and enhancing their livelihoods across districts in Tamil Nadu, Puducherry and the Andaman and Nicobar Islands. Currently, 12,534 farmers are shareholders in these FPCs.

I am proud of this project as it provides ownership to farmers, particularly small and marginal ones who constitute

83 per cent of the shareholder base. Notably, 17 per cent of these farmers are women. Through HIH, we have enabled them to trade ₹21.3 crore through value addition, branding and marketing of their produce.[15]

SUCCESS AT JAWADHU HILLS

The Eastern Ghats are a mountain range in India that spreads across three states—Tamil Nadu, Odisha and Andhra Pradesh. Nestled in a fraction of the Tamil Nadu side in Tiruvannamalai district are the Jawadhu Hills. Famous for its lush sandalwood trees, this region is predominantly inhabited by tribal communities whose sole source of income is farming. Owing to climate change, migration and other factors, livelihoods were fast dwindling here when we started our work in 2008.

In partnership with NABARD and Supraja Foundation, we initiated our interventions here to revive watersheds, recognizing that restoring groundwater levels and creating adequate access would make the next stage of introducing organic farming and other livelihoods easier. The tough terrain coupled with social stigmas faced by tribal communities made it difficult for our team to navigate the early days. But we persisted and have now established our footprint over the last decade, achieving significant milestones, which include doubling farmer incomes, introducing multicropping initiatives and alternative livelihoods, curbing migration and establishing a full-fledged food processing unit.

FARMERS FROM JAWADHU

Kuppusamy's tryst with HIH started as his home was at Kovilur, the site of our first watershed project. His farmland was not fertile and he was living off a meagre income. To introduce him to alternate livelihood options, we initially provided him with four honeybee keeping boxes. A quick learner, he recognized the potential and expanded to 13 boxes in just six months. Within a few years, he was able to harvest a whopping 960 kg of wild honey in its purest form, earning an income of ₹4.8 lakh! With this income, he quickly diversified and invested in cattle worth ₹30,000. This cow produces 2,920 litres of milk annually, adding to his income. Wishing to further diversify his initiatives, Kuppusamy wanted to revive his farmland. We trained him on the potential of mango cultivation for his soil, gave him the necessary inputs and he succeeded with fruit sales too. Kuppusamy did all this at the age of 80; he bought a Honda Activa scooter, which is his biggest milestone yet!

■

Rukku was a landless female farmer, which made her helpless as her husband, Muthu, used to do odd jobs and would leave home for long periods. As a part of our project, we gifted her a cow. With care, training and dedication, she grew it into a small herd and started yielding close to 1,800 litres of milk annually. Rukku's determination and commitment to animal husbandry resulted in a monthly income of ₹54,000. Muthu, impressed with his wife's success, collaborated with her and used a part of the income to lease a small piece of land for cotton farming.

> The cotton yield, almost 100 kg a month, led to a solid monthly income of ₹45,000 for the family of two. They didn't stop there but grew their cotton farm, employing four others and contributing to the development of the economy of the region!
>
> ▪
>
> Finally, let's meet Sivaraji, a farmer with access to land but struggling with dying crops. We introduced him to silver oak plantations and honeybee farming, starting off with 200 plants and two beekeeping boxes, respectively. We also provided pepper seeds, which were sown with the silver oaks intercropping. The pepper started to yield, leading to a harvest of 15 kg a year, which he sells at a rate of ₹450 per kilogram. Before joining our initiative, Sivaraji used to migrate to the neighbouring states of Kerala and Karnataka to support his family, but now he proudly calls Jawadhu home.

Our work in the Jawadhu Hills is a testament to the resilience of the locals and the dedication of my team. Travelling to and from the location takes around four hours and there were barely any facilities for staff when we started our projects. We have now built our own processing centre, dorm and training rooms and this I owe to the passionate team!

HEALTH: REACHING THE UNREACHED

In 2007, I noticed that many of the SHG members were falling behind in their monthly payments for the loans taken, despite being generally good borrowers. A deeper probe revealed that the villages of these women were afflicted with chikungunya, an infection that led to fever and debility for a long period, affecting their income and repayment capacity. I immediately organized medical camps to treat the symptoms early and also to educate on preventive measures. Thus was born the fourth pillar of HIH—health. With support from the government, donors and corporates, HIH started to run general and special camps, including those for malnourished children and women.

Anaemia affects at least 50 per cent women in the rural areas, and children born to anaemic women are generally malnourished and suffer from stunted growth and poor health.[16] HIH launched several initiatives to tackle anaemia and malnutrition, which included food and medical supplements. Poor water quality and sanitation are key factors affecting health and HIH started giving loans to houses for water supply and sanitation with the help of Water.org, resulting in the construction of more than 14,000 toilets.[17] Regular awareness campaigns were conducted to increase awareness of clean water, avoidance of open defecation and improving hygienic conditions in schools.

In 2009, IIT Madras came up with an innovative programme to provide doorstep medical services in remote villages, which led to the establishment of the KaiRaasi Clinic.[18] Each clinic would have a qualified doctor, a paramedic and an assistant. Medicines were donated, and in a few years, the KaiRaasi clinics became popular, serving a significant number of patients, especially those with monthly incomes of less than ₹1,500.

Even though Tamil Nadu has a fairly well-developed health infrastructure, the number of primary health centres was not enough and the KaiRaasi clinics helped in reducing the load on these centres. As part of its focus on children, HIH undertook renovation of anganwadis. Despite being originally built with government money, many of these centres had a dilapidated and foreboding look due to lack of maintenance; HIH modified and improved them to provide welcoming spaces for the children. HIH's approach in this pillar was in tune with its overall objective of supporting public endeavours with private initiative and enthusiasm.

By 2022, HIH had conducted 9,800 medical camps, directly helping about 8,00,000 people and had assisted about 67,000 women with its anaemia control programme, besides bringing about 10,500 children out of malnutrition.[19] In many cases, HIH facilitated access to government services for the poor, supplementing them with additional support and care. The 14 KaiRaasi clinics directly treated about 3,00,000 patients. HIH also renovated about 710 anganwadis, serving as models for successful replication by other agencies.[20]

During the COVID-19 pandemic, HIH diversified its health access model to better serve communities. For instance, HIH established help desks in government hospitals, where thousands of people needing care mill about, largely unaware of what to do and where to go. The help desks quickly reached about 8,40,000 people and helped in creating awareness on the successful vaccination programme of the government. At the same time, in remote areas of Tamil Nadu, Bihar, Jharkhand and Odisha, we started a telemedicine programme.

LENDING A HELPING HAND

Saroja, aged 55, lives in the remote Athipattu village of Kovilur panchayat in Jawadhu Hills, Tamil Nadu. Her husband expired a few years ago and she became the sole breadwinner of the family. She contracted an infection in her left leg while working in her farm. As the nearest government hospital was located 5 km away from her village, she ignored her constant pain and continued her daily chores. When HIH's telemedicine nurse, Ms Bhavani, visited Saroja's village and found her health condition, she immediately took a photo and did a video consultation with our doctor. Based on the doctor's advice, Saroja was referred to a general hospital for further diagnosis. Our staff accompanied her to the hospital and supported her throughout the examination process, which revealed a tumour. Saroja underwent a minor surgery and the tumour was removed successfully.

▪

Rani Kumari, a resident of Nawada, Bihar, found herself married at just 18 years of age to a migrant worker who abandoned her within a few months of marriage. Rani was diagnosed with tuberculosis at 17, but her illness was neglected due to dire poverty and ignorance of family members. This left her with 50 per cent lung damage and severe weight loss. She weighed just 19 kg at 17 years of age!

When our team organized a health camp in her village, we immediately took her to the community health centre to get X-rays and bloodwork done. The results were disturbing as it revealed that she was suffering from severe anaemia and extensive lung damage.

Our team referred her to the TB treatment centre, supporting her financially and also providing rations for one month while she underwent treatment under the National TB Elimination Programme at Sirdala's Primary Health Centre. The treatment was free of cost and provided ₹500 financial assistance for six months. To avail this, our team helped her open a bank account to receive the benefit. HIH has gone beyond just being a healthcare provider and become almost like a family member to Rani, handholding and uplifting her physically and mentally during her recovery. With our support, her health improved and she now weighs 24 kg, a slow and steady improvement.

Stories like Saroja's and Rani's reiterate that our health initiatives have always been about reaching the most remote corners with our health services. Every life transformed is a testament to our mantra of leaving no one behind.

EMPOWERMENT THROUGH SKILL TRAINING AND DEVELOPMENT

2005 was a landmark year in India's journey towards transparency with the enactment of the Right to Information Act, signalling a new era of accessibility and accountability. Well-meaning citizens felt that given India's vast differences in terms of access to information among the citizens, especially from the poor and rural communities, it would be necessary to nurture grassroots-level organizations to take this knowledge-sharing exercise to the people. Organizations like the Catalyst Trust started a Citizens' Centre to disseminate information to the common citizens through educated volunteers by leveraging technology. We collaborated with them and had a successful model for a brief period.

This model later evolved into the Skill Development and Training Centre as right from the beginning, Percy and I were clear that giving cash assistance would not solve anyone's problems and the only way to end poverty is to create as many jobs as possible with the least amount of money so that more and more families would come out of the trap fate had dealt them with.

The skill development pillar emerged as an essential adjunct of HIH's work. We initiated this model through the Aina Tailoring Centre in 2004, which aimed to equip young women above 18 years of age with employable skills in tailoring and then integrating them into the garment industry.

The success of the tailoring venture led HIH to develop many more training programmes offering immediate income opportunities through newly acquired skill sets. Drawing from my experience with the SHGs, I quickly realized the need for specialized entrepreneurship training for these women. This was primarily conducted for women entrepreneurs who had an existing business; they were provided a business development training package, which included modules on basic bookkeeping, business development and marketing. These women expressed desire to upgrade their skills, aspiring to establish microenterprises.

Women from slightly higher-income households pursued training in hobby-related trades such as hand embroidery, cake making and advanced tailoring. HIH found that younger women were eager to learn various skills while older women preferred more traditional skills and wanted HIH to train their younger family members instead.

As of 30 June 2022, nearly 1,61,000 women have received skill training, 2,62,000 digital and financial training and 4,82,000 business development training. We started introducing innovative skill training programmes tailored to the geography, market demand and personal interest of women.[21]

In Madhya Pradesh, training to operate electrical machinery and produce pots was provided to women of a community where men traditionally produced pots. Following this training, women took charge of the production while the men focussed more on sales. This change led to a significant improvement in household incomes.

We also introduced electric-powered tailoring machines, bangle-making machines and bag-making machines, which were traditionally manual tasks. This reduced drudgery, enhanced productivity and increased output for women. The project was supported by Asian Development Bank and helped create energy-based enterprises.

In Tamil Nadu, where literacy rates are higher, women were provided digital training on mobile applications that enabled them to market their products on the internet. This established a digital marketplace where more than 25,000 products were registered, fostering an enterprise ecosystem for women entrepreneurs to expand beyond traditional markets. Furthermore, the women were trained in digital payments, enabling them to grow their businesses without credit risks. Many were also trained to utilize digital platforms such as WhatsApp, Instagram and YouTube for product marketing. A separate training channel was established for this purpose and has more than 3,000 subscribers.[22]

The next target group for HIH's skill development initiatives were the youth. Low availability of appropriately skilled human resources is a problem faced by employers across sectors and locations. The highest skill gaps arise in the most rapidly industrializing areas, where the demand for semi-skilled and skilled manpower is the highest.

Surveys conducted by HIH India indicated that youth aspired for careers in the areas of automobiles, IT and ITeS (information technology enabled services), travel and tourism, retail and BFSI (banking, financial services and insurance). In India, a lot of groundwork had been done by the sector skill councils and the National Skill Development Corporation to develop these skill sets. HIH partnered with such institutions and other educational institutions to provide orientation programmes, relevant skills training, placement opportunities by collaborating with the industry and colleges, certification and career counselling.

HIH mobilized students from rural locations with targeted campaigns conducted by SHGs and community-level organizations. Towards the end of 2021, we realized that many youth had immense potential to contribute towards nation-building but didn't know how to go about training for such examinations. We started the Uniform Service Training programme to provide training for army and police examinations.

One success story from this programme is that of Sasikumar, whose father sold ice at the railway station and mother was a housewife. He had finished his degree and was looking for a job when he joined this programme. After passing the examination, he joined the police academy in Thoothukudi and looks forward to serving the nation with pride.

UNEMPLOYMENT TO NATION-BUILDING

GOKUL'S STORY

What difference can a second make? What difference can an inch make? What difference can a kilogram make? For many it could make or break their career.

I called Gokul early one morning to learn that he had just returned from Uttarakhand. As a proud member of the Indian Army, he had completed three months as a gunner driver, training to handle a gun that can travel 42 km in length and 1 km in radius, along with six others.

This young boy of 22 years from Unai Mottur village in Vellore, Tamil Nadu had attempted the army exams not once or twice but four times. He got rejected in the physical examination every time because he was either a kilogram overweight or his chest size wasn't within the limit or because his sprint timing was just a second slower than required.

Gokul told me, 'My parents have been making and selling *beedi* (local cigarettes) for close to three decades and were certain they didn't want me to join their business. Coming from a neighbourhood in Vellore where there were many retired army officers, it was my father's dream to become an army officer. He couldn't make it, so I made it my ambition.'

Gokul wanted to enrol in coaching classes but the fees were too high. He didn't give up and kept training with his friends. He had one attempt left and that was when HIH launched our first-ever Army Training Course at Vellore. As it was our first course, we ran it for free to gauge interest and see if we would succeed. We roped in an army veteran as the lead trainer and regularly invited officials from the Army, Navy and Air Force to motivate the youth. Our team mobilized 100 youth for the first set of training, but only 40 turned up. Gokul was one of them.

When I asked Gokul about his days of training with us, he gushed, 'Two of the most important things that I took away from the training were firstly, the others I met there. We had such a healthy competition every day and I looked forward to that; and secondly, the importance of structured training to improve our sprint timing and maintain body weight. Our trainer guided us in every exercise meticulously.'

Gokul's dedication and hard work paid off when he successfully passed the selection process on his fifth attempt and underwent rigorous training at Nashik, Maharashtra. Facing linguistic challenges at the training centre, Gokul diligently learnt Hindi alongside his military training, demonstrating his commitment to overcoming obstacles.

'I can now understand close to 70 per cent of Hindi and when I go back, I will reach 100 per cent,' he told me proudly.

Gokul was placed in the Uttarakhand Artillery Unit after the training.

SATISH'S STORY

Hailing from a small village in Pasumpon, Ramanathapuram district of Tamil Nadu, Satish is a young police officer, now married with two kids. He

> is another youth who was trained by our Uniformed Services Training Centre. He had wished to don the police khaki since his childhood. In his first attempt, he failed the written exam by half a mark despite having a perfect score in the physical exam. The second attempt, he passed both with HIH India's help. After passing the examination, he joined as a Grade 2 Armed Reserve Police Officer at Alangulam Police Station, Tenkasi district. He is in training now, where he shadows the other staff in the station and has been on the field, chasing perpetrators and bringing them to the station. He has completed seven months of groundwork and field training. He knows that this is just the beginning and wants to study and become a Sub Inspector.

HIH India's training programme has expanded to two more locations: Athipatti of Virudhunagar district and Kottaimedu (Kamuthi) of Ramnad district. So far, over 100 youth have been trained, with five candidates placed in the army, one in the navy and three in the police.

VILLAGE UPLIFT PROGRAMME

Right from the beginning, a number of institutions and corporates had collaborated with me and HIH as part of their social responsibility ventures. One of the non-negotiables that I followed was collaborating with the government and other institutions in all my endeavours to not replicate what they had already done to ensure economic viability and long-term sustainability.

After the initial rolling out of the five-pillar programme covering CLEP, women empowerment, health, environment and NRM, and skill development, HIH evolved a holistic VUP to address all these aspects within a village. Inspired by Jeffery Sachs' book *The End of Poverty*, this approach was aimed at focussing resources in smaller geographic areas, fostering synergies among the pillars to create model villages.

Under VUP, each village receives about ₹2.5 million to ₹10 million; considering that the Gram Panchayat is the lowest form of civilian government in India, VUP covers all individual villages within a panchayat.

A systematic process is followed in identifying the panchayat and assessing its needs. Local commitment from the villagers and the elected officials is a must to ensure success and sustainability. The interventions are carefully aligned with existing infrastructure created by the government and other institutions, and various committees are formed to ensure community participation in the governance process. For example, if a village needs a pond deepened and protected, a committee of farmers is formed to oversee the work, contribute as needed and later manage it. A school management committee is formed where the local school needs upgradation. In case the village doesn't have a school, the HIH team works with the people to advocate for the establishment of a school by the government. This process involves mobilizing community members to actively participate in Gram Sabhas or village assemblies to gain the attention of the political and government officials to address the issue. As of October 2021, HIH's team had implemented the VUP in 395 villages and was expanding efforts to an additional 70 villages across eight states in India.

HIH has developed a comprehensive process for implementing the VUP activities. The programme begins with a thorough assessment to identify suitable villages based on multiple criteria such as inputs from donors, the strength of village-level institutions, and the willingness of local leaders and residents to actively engage in the programme. The spirit of volunteerism prevalent in the community is essential for ensuring the sustainability of the ventures once HIH leaves the place in about 30 months' time.

Following the identification of target villages, a scoping study is conducted to determine the specific interventions needed, followed by a baseline study to measure outcomes before and after the project. Women empowerment through SHGs and enterprise creation and skill development and training are the two pillars present in all the VUP initiatives while the third pillar is decided based on the unique needs of a village.

❧

The key thrust is one of consensus-building and cooperation so that the existing institutions and knowledge within the community can be fully leveraged. This is facilitated through the establishment of citizen committees, ensuring full participation in all the decision-making processes and fostering ownership of the initiatives; all interventions relevant to the people like health camps, awareness campaigns, linkage with the existing government programmes and developing a corps of volunteers to create a lasting change in the community mindset are undertaken. At the conclusion of the project, an endline study is conducted to assess outcomes and document successes, shortcomings and key learnings. The fact that HIH could get many new VUP's every year is a testament to the effectiveness of the approach.

The other area of partnerships and alliances in which

HIH excelled was in the collaborative ventures with corporates, foundations and other trusts. A few years before the Government of India mandated certain minimum contribution by the corporates for their social responsibility efforts, HIH created a dedicated Partnerships and Alliances team in 2010 to engage with and manage such projects. Companies generally prefer to take up socially impactful near their facilities and partnering with NGOs like HIH allows them to leverage existing connections and expertise without the need to navigate various government agencies and community networks.

A key strength of HIH lies in its integrity and professionalism in adhering to timelines and budgets in addition to undertaking process-oriented measures to validate the impact of the projects. In fact, in many projects, HIH had to contribute its resources to ensure that the targeted outcomes were achieved. This disciplined approach ensures that the HIH team is focussed on identifying community needs, working and engaging with communities more closely and adhering to the discipline of a corporate oversight and audit standards.

Sometimes, the frequent visits of the ever-changing company representatives can take a toll on the time and morale of project teams but overall, the results are considerably more satisfying. In a decade, HIH had collaborated with an average of 50 institutions every year, with an average budget of about ₹75 million to ₹100 million. While Swedish companies and foundations funded many of the projects in the initial years, the majority of funding started coming from Indian entities by 2020.[23]

HIH's model of an integrated approach to poverty alleviation has been built over several years after witnessing the practical difficulties poor people face in the field. I have spent a lot of time every year assessing if the interventions are still relevant, as we too need to change with the times. Each year, my senior team and I convene for a strategic planning meeting to see if we are in alignment with the government vision, field realities and new innovations. Of course, donor funding is a critical aspect, so we try to continue our core programmes along with corporate social responsibility (CSR) projects. With support from several stakeholders, we hope to reach the milestone of creating 10 million jobs by 2025.

The development of our five-pillar model happened sequentially and intuitively. While joining HIH, I thought my focus would be to eliminate child labour but my experiences in the field quickly revealed the multidimensional nature of poverty. It became clear that a multipronged approach was necessary to address its root causes effectively and put an end to it.

As the pillars took shape within the HIH framework, my personal values also consolidated early on. Witnessing the plight of impoverished children instilled in me a deeper empathy and commitment to listen to their views and help them in ways that would truly benefit their lives. The exemplary stories of our women entrepreneurs fuel my determination to do more for society. Our waste management initiatives drove home that change begins in a small way. Similarly, observing the health challenges faced by vulnerable communities due to lack of access or awareness made me feel privileged and grateful for my life, reinforcing my resolve to create an equitable healthcare system for all. Looking at a single pepper tree or paddy field blossom over several years imbibed in me patience and perseverance. It is safe to say that as the pillars evolved, so did I.

9

MY REFLECTIONS

'Dedicating your life to an NGO and creating several organizations to benefit the community is a draining job. No one talks about the high levels of integrity, self-esteem and perseverance you need to get through every day. Some days, the job seems thankless, but you always go to sleep with a content heart—that it is really God's work, service to man!'

—Dr Kalpana Sankar

'Will you do it all over again, if you were given an opportunity?' my daughter asked me when I was working on my book.

'If given a chance I would do it again, but I would do many things differently!' I responded with a smile, remembering the years gone by.

Over the last 20 years, I have had the opportunity to transform lives, visit unique countries, provide jobs to over 13,000 people and touch the lives of over 10 million people globally. But the journey has not been a bed of roses; it has been an uphill task filled with several roadblocks.

One of my most favourite parts of my stint with HIH has been the field visits. I don't have a chance to do it as often now, but when I do, I get a lot of satisfaction from listening to the personal stories of women, children and the community.

When I took up this opportunity in 2004, I had around 10 years of experience in monitoring and evaluation and developing large-scale proposals for institutions like the World Bank. I had the comfort of a government job, exposure to policy-level decision-making and a state-level perspective of the socio-economic landscape.

Joining a grassroots organization was imperative as it offered me direct interaction with the community and acquainted me with a more rigorous field engagement.

I had every intention of going back to my government job after two years. Little did I know that the minute I stepped into the small doorway of Emma House at Kanchipuram, I would be dedicating the rest of my life to this organization.

HIH essentially became my second child, one that I could not abandon for a routine job, one that would challenge me beyond my wildest imagination and one that would grow rapidly and make me ever so proud!

∞

Starting an NGO is not guided by a rulebook; there is no formal manual or institution that prepares founders for the complexities of running a not-for-profit organization. While a degree in development studies or sociology may provide some theoretical knowledge, they don't fully equip you for the statutory, financial, legal and structural realities of managing an NGO.

Passion and empathy will fuel you a little further, but starting an NGO requires practical resources like guidance, legal advice, adequate funding, mentorship and sufficient stakeholder engagement. Acceptance from the community, understanding of social dynamics and building trust are crucial in the early days. These don't come easy and being patient is key, especially in bridging the gap between your perspective and that of the communities you work for.

To truly put yourself in their shoes, you need to visit the field not once or twice but at least 10 times to establish rapport and mutual understanding, with the same motivation and intention in the 10th visit as the first. Forming relationships with the community is the first critical step to building trust, developing the right model and bringing about change.

As important as it is to create a rapport with the community, it is equally important to build a team.

When I joined HIH, the organization had just three other staff members. Finding qualified professionals and convincing them to work in Kanchipuram in a small office, with limited facilities and challenging terrain for upliftment of the poor, was not easy.

One of our first initiatives was the construction of the RSTC in Poongavanam. The first staff I recruited was a civil engineer for this project, followed by a handful of individuals who have been with me since day one. Together, we walked from one household to the next, striving to understand the root causes of child labour and how to eliminate it. These early days allowed me to get my hands dirty and put myself in the shoes of those we aimed to serve.

We were just about 10 people at Emma House—the place

had a posh name but no semblance of an office. I was rather embarrassed that it had more beds than tables and chairs. In 2006, we opened our headquarters with funding from Percy. This gave a visible uplift to the HIH India brand name. We were establishing a premise, a name and visibility for us, and we were here to stay. The new office served as a springboard, attracting qualified staff, but the challenge of sustaining their enthusiasm and ensuring continued salaries always weighed heavily on my mind. I am proud that these staff members have continued with me to this date, deeply committed to HIH India's mission.

*

'Joining an NGO is a lifelong commitment,' I often remind my colleagues and staff, especially those in leadership positions. When you dedicate your entire life to a vision, you can't abandon the job midway or switch off. It is a 24×7 responsibility and is not always fully appreciated.

There were two professional learning curves for me. The first was to adapt to a mentor and leader like Percy, who brought a corporate style of leadership. The second was to understand grassroots-level work and implementing programmes at scale. While I lacked formal mentorship in this area and looked to supporters like the MVF for guidance, I had to ultimately learn on the go.

Beyond professional learnings, there was a personal transformation I needed to undergo to operate better in the system. Although I came from a modestly affluent family, I had to consciously foster a culture of equality at HIH. This meant eating alongside staff and community members during field visits. I remember using aluminium plates at

Isai Ambalam while learning about activity-based learning. While we maintain a title hierarchy for reporting and implementation purposes at HIH, there is no real hierarchy within our organization—everyone is considered equal. This ethos is something I've worked hard to instil in all levels of our NGO.

An NGO not only needs like-minded staff but also a visionary board with integrity and experience to provide guidance when things get tough. It's essential to gather these board members and communicate with them transparently.

To successfully implement project ideas, I first needed capable staff. My team included leaders, grassroots-level mobilizers, a monitoring and evaluation team and a finance team to ensure every impact was measured and every rupee invested yielded results. We had to provide training and continuous learning and development opportunities to keep them interested.

At a deeper level, we need to re-engineer their thought processes. For instance, we had to train our teachers at the RSTCs to never raise their voice at a child however difficult the situation might get. We needed to set high standards and ethics and ensure everyone adhered to those. I am proud that we have sustained at least 1500 people for over 10 years. Continuous mentorship and engagement with the staff, alongside course corrections to keep them aligned with our vision, have been an integral part of the journey. I would call this a path of transformational leadership.

The communities are the custodians of our projects—we operate on their land, in their buildings and for their benefit!

Initially, local bodies were apprehensive about our social development work as their focus was primarily on building and contract work. However, we identified some excellent volunteers—dedicated Child Rights Protection Committee members who were interested in monitoring whether every child was attending school and CLN leaders who focussed on community upliftment.

Our approach became participatory and community-based. We built rapport with local youth and village leaders, which became a cornerstone for sustainability. Training and capacity building along with establishing sustainable local-level institutions helped us understand caste and social dynamics to sync with them mentally and develop meaningful programmes.

Another integral cog in project implementation was the role of the government. We always believed in working in tandem with the government and not create parallel structures. Gaining acceptance from the government is not easy; while some officials are supportive of our model and work with us, others are cold and insulting, making some of our staff feel very small.

Over time, we have learnt to persevere and not lose motivation. I have spent a lot of time counselling my team, providing them courage and encouraging them to reapply with better data or information. I strongly believe that inculcating a sense of confidence amongst the team is essential for creating a resilient cadre of staff.

∞

Throughout my work with HIH, I have always believed in the power of partnerships. With the introduction of the CSR Act, I knew that leveraging corporate partnerships to strengthen public infrastructure would be one way to ensure communities have access to healthcare and education facilities of good standard. In 2016, we started such partnerships and one in particular remains etched in my memory.

In the remote Tiruvannamalai district, Cheyyar Government Hospital required a newborn care unit. With the support of Salcomp, we set up a Sick Newborn Care Unit (SNCU) for treating babies aged one day to one month. The SNCU stands out from the rest of the hospital building. The rooms are equipped with highly advanced equipment resembling those found in private hospitals. The continuous supply of oxygen is ensured through a detailed wall-mounted piping system. The newborns are monitored and attended to round the clock by nurses and doctors. Mothers stay close by in the waiting room and check on their babies every hour. The unit has been functional since March 2016 and has seen a lot of traction, with the average of 40–45 visits per month. There has been a steady drop in referral-outs and increase in referral-ins, which is a big win for the unit.

Apart from treating newborns for illnesses, the nurses and doctors also provide awareness on caring for the children during the first few days by distributing leaflets containing information on feeding and recognizing signs of illnesses.

Based on our assessment findings and requests from the medical team, we have installed an oxygen concentrator in the SNCU. The oxygen concentrator is a critical life-saving device that takes in air and purifies it for those requiring medical oxygen due to low oxygen levels in their blood.

This facility has saved the lives of 1390 children to date and continues its good work![1]

∞

The donor community is fast changing, becoming more scientific and impact-driven. Gone are the days when grants and funds could be used for general development purposes. Each rupee is now tracked by the line item it was intended for. While donors have a stringent due diligence mechanism before onboarding us as their partner, we too conduct a due diligence of the donor to ensure alignment of integrity, culture and values before tying up with them.

Our experiences with donor communities have led us to adopt this approach as many donors base their conclusions on evaluation techniques and impact rather than interacting with the community. Sometimes international agencies come to conclusions without fully understanding the ground realities. We feel the need for stable and passionate donors with a long-term focus and similar strategic goals. We have encountered donors having unrealistic expectations from us or treating us as vendors rather than partners in community development. We have also seen changing in donor attitudes around election times, with priorities shifting and requests for project changes after significant work had been completed on scoping and preparing proposals. My team, both for partnerships and project implementation, bears the brunt of such behaviour for larger public good.

The proof of concept of a proposal becomes visible only a year after project implementation. Change is the only constant and there are new challenges in the field every day. Investing in baseline, midline and endline studies can capture the real situation on the ground. The midline is particularly important for project course correction as field conditions are dynamic. Communication with the donors is critical throughout the process.

Working with multilateral institutions as donors, like

the Asian Development Bank, is a pleasure. Although the paperwork and documentation process can be time consuming, the longer tenure and high-impact projects enable us to bring tangible impact within communities. Since most of these projects also have an impact evaluation component, it gives us solid data-based evidence of our model and work!

It is a known fact that retaining a client is easier than finding a new one. Similarly, retaining a donor is critical in the NGO world. Delivering projects as committed is essential for renewing trust and funding, even though donor priorities may change over time.

There is no room for ego in NGO work. There is a value chain of sorts with donors and the government at the top along with the community and NGOs at the bottom. For instance, while NGOs may believe they are doing phenomenal work, community buy-in is essential. If the community is instigated to turn against you, it becomes a huge challenge. We should remember that the outcome is not under our control, but the process is. The governments and corporates also have their own agendas, which may not always align with community needs. We, as the NGO, often find ourselves in the middle of this trifecta.

In such situations, we should be firm in our non-negotiables, flexible in our approach and strategy and willing to shed our ego when dealing with stakeholders! Humility and patience are two key attributes needed in the social sector and honestly, these don't develop overnight. Accountability is paramount when receiving funds from donors and we must have utmost patience.

These are some principles that I was fortunate to learn from my mentors, Dr H. Sudarshan and Mr Venkat Reddy, and I strive to instil these principles in my staff, encouraging them to work and live by them.

~

For HIH, the ultimate goal is job creation. While we receive donor funding for training and mobilization of women, the crucial link of credit support for them to establish their enterprises was always a challenge. This gap was addressed by banks and NBFCs, prompting me to set up Belstar with a vision to extend this offering as a part of the HIH network.

One of Belstar's investors is the Sarvam Mutual Benefit Trust, comprising share capital from thousands of SHG women. All was well but when the Andhra Pradesh microfinance crisis struck, the entire industry developed cold feet and was hesitant to support Belstar. Prior to this, it was common for MFIs to take contributions from local women for equity, but the crisis led to severe criticism and reluctance among investors to accept community contribution as equity.

Hailing from a conservative family that didn't have generational wealth, it was an uphill battle to come out of this situation. It was at this critical time that the Trustees of HIH gave me support and strength. With their guidance and approval, we secured a loan from a local bank, enabling us to pay the women fair value for their contributions and got a clean chit from CRISIL to continue operations! The bank loan was repaid after offloading shares during secondary investment.

~

The resplendent Swedish west coast with its pristine blue waters, the rugged terrain of South African cape, the lively promenade at Rio De Janerio, the hallowed classrooms at HBS, dolphins in the Mekong and the prestigious Durbar Hall at the Rashtrapati Bhavan—I have seen it all!

I have also witnessed the favelas of Rio, shanty towns just off Durban in South Africa, the impoverished households at Phnom Penh and abject poverty in rural India. Travel, both within India and globally, has opened my eyes to the stark inequality between the West and the developing countries. The perspective we gain from India is vastly different from what Africa and South America face, and each location required a customized solution. Our global replication phase involved a lot of personal risk for me as I had to work in difficult conditions without personal security, insurance or even sufficient travel allowance. Each trip was a learning experience and I ensured that all my staff had insurance and travel allowance during their trips to avoid putting them or their families through any hardship.

In South Africa, even inside the hotel, there would be moments where I had to run for my life due to harassment. But problems started even before I had reached our hotel. Madhu and I had travelled together to South Africa the first time. We were standing in separate lines during immigration. She crossed the counter with no hassle but the officer looked at me and my passport multiple times, making me wait endlessly. The reason was that he could not read the visa properly as it was not 'clear' according to him. It was a legitimate passport and visa stamped by the authorities in India. I felt helpless, claustrophobic and nauseous. After nearly 20 minutes of waiting, he finally took pity on me and allowed me to proceed.

Reflecting on South Africa, another memory stands out. I was about to address a grand audience led by a minister when my daughter, Sahaana, called me. She was in India, studying in class eight, and had received disappointing results in her math exam. Oblivious to the importance of my meeting, she asked me, 'Why did I do so badly, Amma?' The guilt I felt that day for not being with my daughter to comfort her or to help her with her study haunted me and I questioned myself whether I was doing the right thing.

My visit to China presented numerous challenges as everything was new and in Mandarin, and there were very few English speakers. Being a vegetarian also added to the challenge. Similarly in Vietnam, I struggled without coffee for 10 days. Little did I know that they didn't have coffee or milk. In Turin, Italy, I found myself feeling isolated as I was the sole representative from HIH whereas representatives of other organizations had come in groups of three or four. After this experience, I always ensured my staff travelled in teams for trainings!

My visits highlighted that the fundamental ideology of fundraising and poverty work in the West was polar opposite of how grassroots organizations in India perceive it. Westerners visiting India often lack an understanding of local context, caste dynamics and field realities. But after the visits, their approach for fundraising, which included lavish parties and galas at big hotels surprised me. I kept thinking of how that money could have been used to help the poor.

In India, we value simplicity and transparency. Nevertheless, over time, I too understood the importance of presenting our work globally to create awareness and have opportunities to replicate our model in different regions. This learning process, though challenging, taught me how to adapt my attire, speech, and conduct to navigate Western settings effectively.

My first trip to Sweden was in April 2006. Assuming spring would be manageable and not that chilly, I just packed a couple of sweaters. The weather caught me off guard as I was not used to such cold temperatures. Percy showed his fatherly side and lent me his coat. I will never forget this warm gesture. Subsequent visits to Sweden and other Western countries found me better prepared for the weather, equipped with appropriate clothing and shoes.

During one such trip to Sweden with Percy for a presentation at Globeforum, the airline lost my baggage upon arrival. With few shops open on a Sunday, I faced the challenge of finding clothes that fit my 'Indian' body shape. How you look directly translates to your confidence levels, especially in a foreign land! Thankfully, I managed to find something on Monday and a colleague helped me sew the pants to fit me well. The meeting was a success!

My experiences in New York, London and Paris during my TRIUM course were rather insightful. My classmates, mostly affluent business leaders, had resplendent wardrobes while I had one winter coat to see me through 14 days. I needed to keep up, so I saved on food expenses by cooking one meal in the hotel room and spending on clothes and accessories to help me feel more accepted. I knew that I matched everyone in intelligence and my experience in the classroom spoke volumes, but for my voice to be heard, I knew I had to keep up my external appearance. These travels also made me focus more on my physical fitness—for health reasons but also to fit into size 10 or 12 dresses and pants! I hired a personal coach to guide me on grooming and presentation—this gave me confidence.

As an Indian woman from a conservative household, adapting to new habits and cultural norms during my travels was a journey in itself. While I loved rice, it wasn't always an option, and mastering chopsticks was a skill I had to acquire as everyone around me was adept at it. Even networking in parties, staying out late in the night without my family or husband, was something I was not used to. I was hardworking and knew I could implement a project well and defend it, but dressing for the role and promoting it amongst billionaires with confidence was a cultural adaptation to the West that I embraced. Sometimes, I was disheartened by how India was being perceived through a myopic lens in the West; poverty seemed to be a constant subject of ridicule over drinks. However, I always maintained dignity while explaining the reality and the root causes of poverty and how one could lend their support for the cause.

My courses abroad further honed my confidence as I encountered some phenomenal individuals who, despite their simplicity, made significant contributions to the world. Figures like Prof. Kash Rangan of HBS, Prof. Ashwath Damodaran of NYU, Liz, Ann and Amanda of the East-West Center, Mary and Naomi of TRIUM and Hans Wahl of INSEAD. Even though they came from the world of academia, they had acclimatized themselves to the fundraising space exceptionally well. I strove to follow their footsteps and carve a niche for me, hoping to make a difference and build progressive communities.

❧

In 2007, when I was at the Pietermaritzburg Station in South Africa, I couldn't hold back my tears. I thought about how

Mahatma Gandhi's vision of Satyagraha was born and imagined his tough night in the bitter winter he spent at the station. It was then that I decided to carry on with a renewed fire despite the hiccups along the way!

The challenges that I faced have only led to personal growth. I am a different person today than I was when I began this journey. Every experience has been a learning moment that refined my interactions with everyone around me. I learnt early on from Percy to never send emails when angry. It is always more effective to talk and clarify instead of typing impulsively. I have learnt to be more forgiving and value goodness, which exists in all of us. We must learn to forgive and move on without compromising on integrity and values. My family and some senior colleagues have been pillars of strength and support, especially in challenging times. While receiving international and national awards, several will congratulate, but very few stick by during the hard times when slander, misinformation and false propaganda prevail. One has to keep going despite the challenges and upheavals.

EPILOGUE

9 MARCH 2019, NEW YORK

As I draped my sari on a chilly winter morning at the Millennium Hotel, just adjacent to the UN Headquarters in New York, my mind raced with a myriad of emotions, nostalgia and gratitude.

I was here with Sankar and Sahaana to receive the prestigious Princess Sabeeka Bint Ibrahim Al Khalifa Award for Women Empowerment under the Individual Champions Category. Presented by UN Women and the Kingdom of Bahrain in the beautiful ECOSOC Chambers of the UN Headquarters, it was a crowning moment for my work towards women empowerment through HIH and Belstar. As I felt humbled at the thought of greats like M.S. Subbulakshmi representing India at the UN in the past, I once again reflected on my journey.

From a research scientist in Nuclear Physics to delving into Gender Studies, I transitioned to working in a school in between and raised my family. My path led me to projects on women empowerment and poverty elimination within the government. Joining HIH provided my first exposure to a grassroots-level rural organization. Overtime, I was catapulted to collaborate with an international business tycoon who had run massive enterprises with thousands of employees worldwide.

Eventually, I started a microfinance company with practically no experience in corporate affairs. Equipping myself with an international Executive MBA programme, I found myself sitting in classes alongside CEOs and chief financial officers of global companies. I travelled to Afghanistan, Brazil, South Africa, Cambodia, Myanmar and Sri Lanka, advocating our model and often being the only woman in the room but at the head of the table.

I believe that any woman can achieve such feats by applying herself to the task! Believing in yourself and constantly equipping your skills has been my go-to. Here are a few closing thoughts that may help you achieve everything you set out to do.

So, here it goes:

Commitment and sensitivity come naturally to women. My first suggestion would be to find something that you are passionate about. I have always been passionate about empowerment, welfare of children and addressing poverty sustainably. Yours could be fashion design, clothing, footwear, health and nutrition, education, special children, environment, catering or anything. What matters is that you must have the passion to excel and strive constantly in that sphere.

To this day, I believe that it is important to constantly upskill yourself. I am constantly equipping myself. I recently attended a programme on Competent Boards run by Canadian professors and practitioners to be abreast of ESG (environmental, social and governance) and its importance in a board context. All these have given fresh insights into running our enterprises well and in catering better to the expectations of the donors and institutions. They have also helped me in challenging existing practices and views and broadened my understanding.

I attended special coaching classes with British Council in India to develop my oratory skills and improved my reading habits to cover a wide range of topics, which helped me gain a better perspective on future trends.

Being the only woman in a corporate boardroom, you need to be attentive, well informed and should be able to convey your thoughts in a cogent and assertive manner. While your performance would stand in good stead always, certain issues need skilful negotiation. It may be difficult to have your way all the time. Experience teaches you how to weather most of these issues skilfully.

The boards of both HIH and Belstar have taught me to be more humble, effective and true to myself. Being a research scientist, I have been very particular about documenting my work and in engaging with academic institutions like the IIT, IIM and many more, which helps us to improve our functioning. We are quite active on social media and our monthly newsletters convey a wealth of information like clockwork and keep our focus. We are responsive to adverse comments and maintain our professional approach even if we know that the comments are sometimes motivated.

A true leader would not be floored by the bouquets or brickbats. Women leaders have to extend their communication to conferences, media interviews and finding time to attend policy-level discussions, especially with institutions like the RBI.

The last point I would like to convey is that as a leader,

you must constantly be prepared for the worst and have contingency plans all the time. This is more so when things appear to be especially good. Periodic reviews and peer or external evaluations would help in anticipating the fault lines and prepare accordingly. This also requires that you shed all non-critical functions to efficient subordinates and concentrate on the big picture. Financial discipline is important but if you spend most of your time on budgets and approvals, you won't have the time to anticipate. Keeping skip-level communication channels open is necessary to plan for the unplanned.

My quick responses have sometimes led to problems, but overall, they have helped the organization. I am accessible 24×7 for critical inputs and my immediate team knows that escalating an issue should only occur if solutions are not amicably found by them. Over time, you gain the ability to be non-judgemental in your handling of people and in HIH, right from the beginning, we have been working on our operational strategy for at least a five-year term so that we remain focussed in our areas of thrust while leaving sufficient buffer for unforeseen events.

Life has a strange way of throwing opportunities and curveballs at you. I believe I have learnt from both. I hope you have taken away something meaningful from my story and are inspired to create impact in your life!

ACKNOWLEDGEMENTS

I am a deeply spiritual person who believes that a greater power blesses our every action. I thank God for his abundant blessings in my personal and professional life.

HIH would not be what it is and there would be no story to write about if not for Percy. I thank him for trusting me on that balmy summer day in Kanchipuram, allowing me to witness his enormous wisdom and processes in running institutions and setting the goalpost high. I am grateful to him for providing a foreword for this book.

HIH's Board of Trustees has been always a sounding board and guiding light during ups and downs. I am ever grateful for their unflinching support and trust in my work.

HIH's achievements and accolades go to my sincere and dedicated team who are available 24×7 for the children and women we work with. Their collaborative efforts have created the impact that has allowed me to pen several chapters in this book.

Belstar started as a whim after my training course at Boulder. I extend my gratitude to the Managing Director of Muthoot Finance, Mr George Alexander Muthoot, for his timely strategic intervention in Belstar and for inspiring me to create a company with an asset base of over ₹10,000 crores. My team at Belstar has risen to every occasion and I am grateful for their positive attitude and resilience.

Prof. Kash Rangan of Harvard Business School and Prof. Ashwath Damodaran of NYU Stern School of Business have been inspiring teachers who I look up to. Their reviews of my book have only reiterated my success. I thank all my professors in every cohort I have been a part of—TRIUM, HBS-Accion and INSEAD—for igniting a spark in me to return home and be a better version of myself. I thank Ms Leena Nair, IAS (Retd.), a civil servant and my boss at the Tamil Nadu Women's Development Corporation, for her support and encouragement in the early days of my career.

Rajeshwari Swaminathan's proactive approach in highlighting my entrepreneurial journey to the world of publishers and editors has really put me on the literary map. Vini Bhati, my editorial consultant, has been a sheer pleasure to work with over the past several months. Her crystal-clear thought process and feedback on the initial versions of the manuscript have been pivotal in bringing out the final version that you have with you today. I thank Dibakar Ghosh of Rupa Publications for believing in my story and bringing it to print. I also thank Anupama Roy, my editor at Rupa, for refining the rough edges and making the manuscript whole!

I want to thank my parents for their love and instilling in me the grit to pursue anything I set my heart on. My sisters and my son-in-law Srashta have been pillars of strength in my entrepreneurial journey and I can't wait for them to read this book.

Sahaana, my daughter, has been working with me professionally for the last eight years. She has been responsible for editing, reviewing, reading and re-reading this manuscript for the last year, adding value in every page and paragraph. Thank you, Sahu, for being my loudest cheerleader.

Finally, I want to thank my husband, Sankar. It was he who started documenting my journey by reviewing and scouring hundreds of memos, pages of notes and booklets from my early days when we were in the middle of the COVID-19 lockdown. His initial draft has been the source code for this entire manuscript coming together. Thank you, Sankar, for celebrating me and my achievements like your own.

ABBREVIATIONS

AREDP	Afghanistan Rural Enterprise Development Programme
CEO	Chief Executive Officer
CLEP	Child Labour Elimination Programme
CLN	Cluster-level Network
COO	Chief Operating Officer
CRDT	Cambodian Rural Development Team
ECOSOC	Economic and Social Council
FPC	Farmer Producer Company
HIH	Hand in Hand (India)
HIH SA	Hand in Hand South Africa
HIHAO	Hand in Hand Afghanistan Organization
HIHCSPL	Hand in Hand Consulting Services Pvt Ltd
HIHMFL	Hand in Hand Microfinance Ltd
IDB	Inter-American Development Bank
IFAD	International Fund for Agricultural Development
IIC	International Investment Council
IIM	Indian Institute of Management
IIT	Indian Institute of Technology
LSE	London School of Economics

MIF	Multilateral Investment Fund
MRRD	Ministry of Rural Rehabilitation and Development
MUCPP	Mangaung-University Community Partnership Programme
NABARD	National Bank for Agriculture and Rural Development
NBFC	Non-banking Finance Company
NGO	Non-government Organization
REDES	Reduction of Poverty through Regional Integration of Local Business Capacities
SCG	Savings Credit Group
SHG	Self-help Group
SIDBI	Small Industries Development Bank of India
UN	United Nations
VUP	Village Uplift Programme

NOTES

PROLOGUE

1. Hand in Hand India, *Monthly Report*, September 2023.
2. Hand in Hand India, *Monthly Report*, May 2024.
3. Sachs, Jeffrey D., *The End of Poverty*, The Penguin Press, New York, 2005.
4. HIH worked with government schools to provide training to the teachers, prepare extra material for students to cope with the syllabus and improve school infrastructure. This intervention is called the 'school strengthening programme'.

CHAPTER 3: THE INITIAL STRUGGLES

1. *Head Accountant Report*, 2002–2003.
2. Barnevik, Percy, *Review of Hand in Hand's Activities*, 23 October 2003.
3. Hand in Hand (Sweden) Tamil Nadu, *Annual Report 2003–2004*.
4. Amount as revealed to Dr Kalpana Sankar by former employee Mr Rex Vazz.

5. 'RIVER - Institute for Educational Resources,' *RISHI VALLEY EDUCATION CENTRE*, https://www.rishivalley.org/river-institute-for-educational-resources. Accessed on 26 May 2024.

CHAPTER 4: TACKLING MULTIDIMENSIONAL POVERTY

1. Grameen Foundation, https://grameenfoundation.org/about-us/why-grameen. Accessed on 26 May 2024.
2. IFAD, *Tamil Nadu Women's Development Project*, https://www.ifad.org/en/web/operations/-/project/1100000240. Accessed on 26 May 2024.
3. Sankar, Kalpana, *4th Board Meeting Agenda and Minutes dated 11.04.2005*, Hand in Hand Tamil Nadu.
4. Hand in Hand India, *Annual Report 2004-2005* and *Board Agenda Notes 2004-2005*.
5. Hand in Hand (Sweden) Tamil Nadu, *Annual Report 2003-2004* and Hand in Hand Tamil Nadu, *Agenda Notes*, April, 2005.

CHAPTER 5: THE GLOBAL FOOTPRINTS

1. Hand in Hand Tamil Nadu, *Annual Report 2006-07*.
2. Sankar, Kalpana, *4th Board Meeting Agenda and Minutes dated 11.04.2005*, Hand in Hand Tamil Nadu.
3. South-South Cooperation is a collaboration of the Global South (developing countries) through which they 'share knowledge, skills, expertise and resources to meet their development goals through concerted efforts' Source: 'South-South Cooperation Day,' *United Nations*, https://www.un.org/en/observances/south-south-cooperation-day. Accessed on 27 May 2024.

4. Gumede, Vusi, *Poverty and the 'Second Economy' in South Africa: An Attempt to Clarify Applicable Concepts and Quantify Extent of Relevant Challenges,* 2008, https://doi.org/10.2139/ssrn.1360771.
5. MoU between *Hand in Hand* and *The Independent Development Trust* for the 'Accelerated Shared Growth Initiative of South Africa: Jobs for Growth Programme', August 2006.
6. MoU between *Mangaung University of the Free State Community Partnership Programme,* Free State, Republic of South Africa and *Hand in Hand,* Tamil Nadu, India, August 2007.
7. The model provides access to finance to people living in poverty in rural and hard-to-reach areas.
8. Sankar, Kalpana, Revolving Fund for Startups//Pilots, 2006.
9. ToR between *Hand in Hand Microfinance Ltd* and *Hand in Hand Southern Africa,* November 2012.
10. World Population Review, https://worldpopulationreview.com/country-rankings/gender-equality-by-country. Accessed on 26 May 2024.
11. United Nations, *HUMAN DEVELOPMENT REPORT 2009, UNDP,* https://www.undp.org/sites/g/files/zskgke326/files/migration/tr/J-Gender-related-development-index-and-its-components.pdf. Accessed on 27 May 2024.
12. Dutta, Mondira, *Initiatives for Afghan Women:* sponsored by the Ministry of External Affairs, Government of India, 2010.
13. Hand in Hand India, *Annual Report 2007–08: Message from our CEO and Advisor,* 2007–08.
14. *Poverty Alleviation Through Livelihoods: Insights from Global Experience,* Hand in Hand Consulting Services Publication.

15. Dutta, Mondira, *Initiatives for Afghan Women:* sponsored by the Ministry of External Affairs, Government of India, 2010.
16. Ibid.
17. Prasad, Jayant, 'Don't Forget Afghans: As Kabul Gets a New Regime, GoI Must Maintain People Contact and Not Squander Hard-Won Goodwill,' *Times of India Blog,* 1 September 2021, https://timesofindia.indiatimes.com/blogs/toi-edit-page/india-dont-forget-afghans-as-kabul-gets-a-new-regime-goi-must-maintain-people-contact-and-not-squander-hard-won-goodwill/?utm_source=facebook.com&utm_medium=social&utm_campaign=TOI. Accessed on 26 May 2024.
18. Inter-American Development Bank, https://www.iadb.org/en/who-we-are/about-idb. Accessed on 27 May 2024.
19. Sandoval, Lindsay, et al., 'The Effect of Education on Brazil's Economic Development,' *Global Majority E-Journal,* Vol. 3, No. 1, June 2012, 4–19, https://www.american.edu/cas/economics/ejournal/upload/sandoval_accessible.pdf. Accessed on 27 May 2024.
20. Hand in Hand Microfinance Services, *Preliminary Report of MD,* 2008.
21. Hand in Hand India, https://hihindia.org/global-presence/brazil/. Accessed on 27 May 2024.
22. 'Poverty Reduction Thu Regional Integration of Local Capacities of Integral Dev,' *IDB,* 30 April 2024, https://www.iadb.org/en/whats-our-impact/RG-M1145. Accessed on 27 May 2024.
23. Letter of Understanding between *Hand in Hand Microfinance Ltd* and *World Vision,* Guatemala, July 2011.
24. In rural areas where there weren't many hospitals, it was common to see intravenous drips hanging from mango

tree branches to be administered in case of an emergency.

25. Pimhidzai, Obert, et al., *Microfinance and Household Welfare: Cambodia Policy Note*. World Bank Group, 2019. https://documents1.worldbank.org/curated/en/144661552916327946/pdf/128266-REVISED-WP-PUBLIC-Nota-MFI-web.pdf. Accessed on 27 May 2024.
26. *Poverty Alleviation Through Livelihoods: Insights from Global Experience,* Hand in Hand Consulting Services Publication.
27. Ibid.
28. Value chain formation and training included an end-to-end process on introduction to the crop, cultivation, harvest and connecting to market to ensure there is no productivity loss at every step.
29. Krishnaswamy, Karuna, *Evaluation of the Self-Help Group and Microfinance-Based Livelihood Project of Asian Institute of Technology, Cambodia Rural Development Team & Hand in Hand India,* Independent Consultant, June 2013.
30. Certificate of Registration as Rural Credit Institution, National Bank of Cambodia, 2019.
31. Hand in Hand Consulting Services Pvt Ltd, *Endline Evaluation Report, Cambodia SHG Project for increased Livelihood (CSPL),* November 2021.
32. *Poverty Alleviation Through Livelihoods: Insights from Global Experience,* Hand in Hand Consulting Services Publication.
33. Ibid.
34. Ibid.
35. 'Poverty: Overview', *World Bank,* https://www.worldbank.org/en/topic/poverty/overview. Accessed on 27 May 2024.

CHAPTER 6: CREATIVE INSTITUTION BUILDING

1. Hand in Hand Microfinance Pvt Ltd, *Annual Report 2008-09.*
2. 'The Companies Act, 2013', *mca.gov.in*, p. 28, https://www.mca.gov.in/Ministry/pdf/CompaniesAct2013.pdf. Accessed on 27 May 2024.
3. 'TN's Bio-gas Project on BBC Award Shortlist', *The New Indian Express*, 17 May 2012, https://www.newindianexpress.com/cities/chennai/2011/Oct/21/tns-bio-gas-project-on-bbc-award-shortlist-302474.html. Accessed on 27 May 2024.
4. 'UNEP Announces Winners of World Environment Day Challenge', *SDG KNOWLEDGE HUB: A Project by IISD*, https://sdg.iisd.org/news/unep-announces-winners-of-world-environment-day-challenge/. Accessed on 27 May 2024.
5. Belstar Microfinance Limited, *Annual Report 2021–22*, https://belstar.in/annual-reports/. Accessed on 27 May 2024.
6. Department of Agriculture & Farmers Welfare, *Annual Reports*, https://agriwelfare.gov.in/en/Annual. Accessed on 27 May 2024.
7. Indian Natural Farmers Producers Company Pvt Ltd, *Annual Report 2020–21.*
8. Permanent Mission of Switzerland to the United Nations Office and to the Other International Organizations in Geneva data, 2023.

CHAPTER 7: SHARPENING THE SAW

1. Hand in Hand India, *Annual Report 2008–09.*
2. Sriram, M.S., 'The AP Microfinance Crisis 2010: Discipline or Death?,' *Vikalpa: The Journal for Decision Makers,* Vol. 37, No. 4, 1 October 2012, 113–28, https://doi.org/10.1177/0256090920120407. Accessed on 27 May 2024.
3. Gopalswamy, Arun Kumar, et al., *SROI Assessment for Hand in Hand,* Indian Institute of Technology Madras, 2015.
4. Lerpold, Lin, et al., *SSE Teaching Case,* Hand in Hand India, 2008.
5. Sriram, M.S., *Belstar India Finance,* Indian Institute of Management Bangalore, 18 January 2018, https://hbsp.harvard.edu/product/IMB661-PDF-ENG. Accessed 27 May 2024.
6. Adams, Annie, et al., *Hand in Hand India: Case No. E372,* Stanford Graduate School of Business, 2009.
7. Saluja, Rashmi, 'The Year 2024 Belongs to Women-led Startups and Entrepreneurs,' *ETBFSI.com,* 27 January 2024. https://bfsi.economictimes.indiatimes.com/blog/the-year-2024-belongs-to-women-led-startups-and-entrepreneurs/107177301. Accessed on 27 May 2024.
8. 'The Companies Act, 2013,' *mca.gov.in,* p. 98, https://www.mca.gov.in/Ministry/pdf/CompaniesAct2013.pdf. Accessed on 5 June 2024.
9. Kumari, Jagriti, 'Women's Representation in Leadership Roles Soars,' *People Matters,* 14 August 2023, https://www.peoplematters.in/news/diversity/womens-representation-in-leadership-roles-soars-38701. Accessed on 27 May 2024.

CHAPTER 8: THE FIVE PILLARS OF HAND IN HAND

1. 'Approach,' *M VENKATARANGAIYA FOUNDATION*, https://mvfindia.in/approach/. Accessed on 27 May 2024.
2. Isai Ambalam School, https://isaiambalamschool.wordpress.com/. Accessed on 27 May 2024.
3. Hand in Hand India, *Annual Report 2021–22.*
4. An administrative circle under a district, similar to a tehsil.
5. Vodafone-Indus Towers supported RISE App project with Hand in Hand India report.
6. Hand in Hand India, *Annual Report 2021–22* & Belstar Microfinance, *Annual Report 2021–22.*
7. Hand in Hand India, Monthly Report, May 2024.
8. Gopalswamy, Arun Kumar, et al., *SROI Assessment for Hand in Hand*, Indian Institute of Technology Madras, 2015.
9. Malegam, Y. H., *Report of the Sub-Committee of the Central Board of Directors of Reserve Bank of India to Study Issues and Concerns in the MFI Sector*, January 2011.
10. Chintan Environmental Research and Action Group, *Wastepickers: Delhi's Forgotten Environmentalists?*, 2019, https://www.chintan-india.org/sites/default/files/2019-09/Supreme%20Court%20Report_01.pdf. Accessed on 27 May 2024.
11. Hand in Hand India, *Annual Report 2021–22.*
12. Anu Hasan & Muniyammal - Strong Women in Conversation, YouTube, 5 May 2020, https://www.youtube.com/watch?v=YDdDoJ5NIP4. Accessed on 27 May 2024.
13. Hand in Hand India, *Annual Report 2021–22.*
14. Saha Soumen, et al., 'Non-iron Deficiency Anemia in Rural Indian Women: A Cross-Sectional Study,' *Cureus*, 29 Aug 2022, https://www.cureus.com/articles/111948-non-

iron-deficiency-anemia-in-rural-indian-women-a-cross-sectional-study#!/. Accessed on 27 May 2024.

15. Hand in Hand India *Project Completion Report for Water.org*, 2016.
16. Hand in Hand India, *Annual Report 2009–10*, Article by Prof. Thillai Rajan, IIT Madras.
17. Hand in Hand India, *Annual Report 2021–22.*
18. Ibid.
19. Ibid.
20. YouTube, https://www.youtube.com/@ThozhilKalam360/featured. Accessed on 6 June 2024.
21. Hand in Hand India, *Annual Report 2021–22.*
22. Ibid.
23. Hand in Hand India, Reports for NABARD.

CHAPTER 9: MY REFLECTIONS

1. Hand in Hand India, *SNCU Report 2019.*